VEGETABLES
COOKBOOK

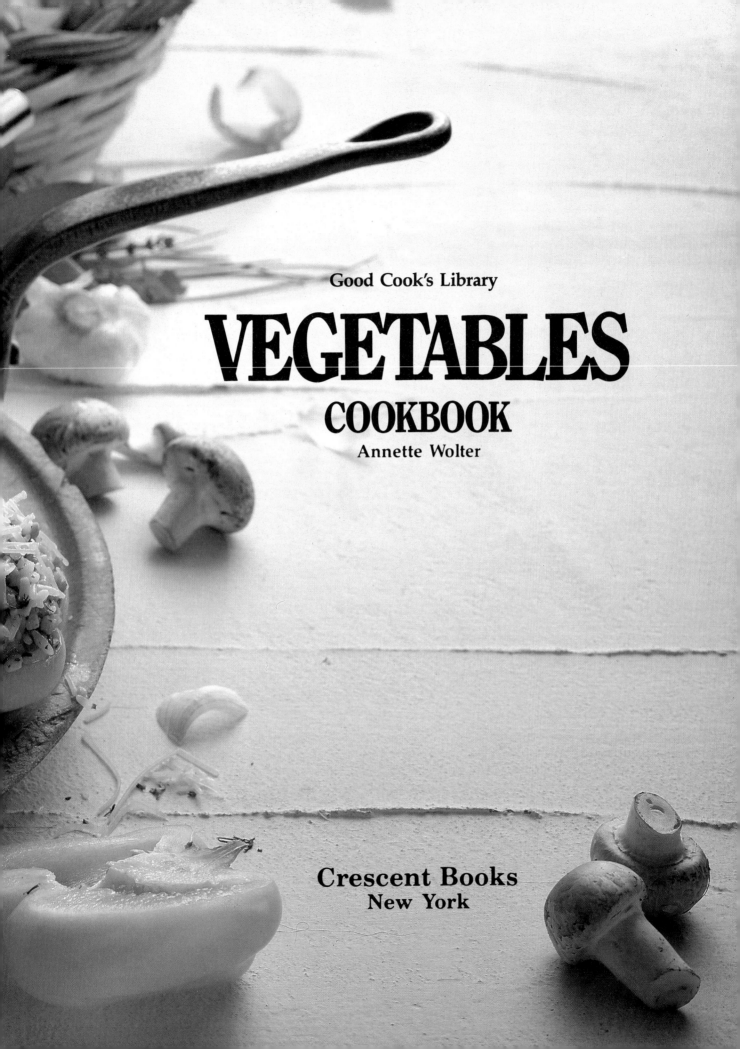

Good Cook's Library

VEGETABLES
COOKBOOK
Annette Wolter

Crescent Books
New York

Contents

About this Book

Fresh vegetables are a boundless resource for the creative cook. Fresh vegetables are high in vitamins and minerals and low in calories. They are a first choice for flavor, ease in preparation and food value.

A wide variety of delicious dishes prepared with vegetables are found in this cookbook. Each recipe is accompanied by a full-color photograph. Not only well-known dishes such as stuffed peppers or stuffed cabbage leaves are featured, but lesser known recipes are included. Vegetable soufflés, marinated vegetables, hearty vegetable casseroles, purees, Swiss chard cake, zucchini quiche and artichoke pizza are some of the mouth-watering recipes in this book.

Tips for selecting and purchasing vegetables, step-by-step instructions for cooking vegetables and the large number of recipes makes it easy to find the best dish for any occasion.

Chapter One includes vegetable soups, appetizers and light dishes. Chapter Two is devoted to vegetable recipes that can serve as complete meals or to complete a light meat, fish or poultry course. These recipes combine meat, fish or poultry with the vegetable. Many interesting combinations are presented. A wide array of tempting salads are presented in Chapter Three. These are both warm and cold salads of usual and unusual combinations.

International vegetable specialties are described in the final chapter. Included are such dishes as Russian borscht, Alsatian sauerkraut, Mediterranean ratatouille, Mexican chili con carne and Turkish pan-fried eggplant.

Preparation methods are described in an easy-to-follow manner. Both the gourmet and inexperienced cook will enjoy this book. Preparation and cooking times and the number of calories have been included for each dish.

All recipes are for 4 servings unless otherwise indicated.

The Value of Vegetables

Vegetables taste good and contain valuable nutrients. Vegetables must be selected carefully, stored properly and prepared with care.

Perfect shape and large size are not necessarily an indication of quality. This perfection is often achieved by chemical treatment and fertilizers, which can leave large residues of harmful substances in the plants. For the freshest vegetables, choose locally grown vegetables. Organically grown vegetables are grown without mineral fertilizers and chemical pesticides. While they are not as attractive as non-organically grown vegetables, they are an excellent choice. Fresh vegetables should be prepared soon after purchase.

Trimming is the first step in the preparation of vegetables. Roots need to be removed and other parts of the vegetable discarded, such as the outer leaves of cabbages and the dark green tops of leek leaves.

Trimmed vegetables should always be thoroughly washed. Rinse tender leaf vegetables by turning frequently under a gentle stream of water. Scrub smooth-skinned vegetables well while rinsing under running water. Brush rough surfaces caked with soil thoroughly while holding under running water. Remove coarse and tough stems as well as spoiled leaves from leaf vegetables and herbs. A salad spinner will remove excess water from leafy vegetables.

Tubers such as carrots, turnips and celeriac should be scraped with a knife blade or peeled. Pull off the thin, outer, fibrous skin from asparagus and celery. To

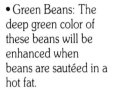

peel tomatoes and peppers easily, dip them in boiling water until the skin bursts, or heat under the broiler until skin is charred and is easily removed. Cut or tear off inedible parts such as stems and strings. Do not rinse vegetables again or soak them in water, since valuable nutrients will be lost. Always cook vegetables for the shortest possible period of time at the lowest possible temperature. Many vegetables can be eaten raw as raw vegetables contain more nutrients than cooked ones. Reserve one-third of the raw vegetable requested in the recipe, grate it and mix into the cooked portion just before serving.

Use the cooking method that requires the least amount of liquid. A small number of vegetables, such as asparagus, are usu-

ally steamed. The lightly salted steaming water can be used in a soup. Various step-by-step cooking methods are shown on the next four pages.

The following is a potpourri of tips and terms about various vegetables:

• Artichokes: Do not cook artichokes in an aluminum pan because the aluminum will discolor the artichokes and give them a metallic taste.

• Cauliflower: Add salt after cooking cauliflower as salt causes the florets to discolor. For a milder flavor, cook cauliflower in an equal amount of milk and water.

• Cucumbers: Some cucumbers are bitter near the stem end. Cut a small slice from the stem end before preparing the cucumber.

• Eggplant: For a milder flavor, slice washed eggplant lengthwise, sprinkle with salt and set aside for 15 minutes to allow the salt to draw the excess water from the eggplant. Rinse the slices with cold water, blot dry and continue as indicated in the recipe.

• Fennel: Immediately sprinkle cut fennel with lemon juice to avoid discoloration. Cut fennel into julienne strips, or grate it and use raw in tossed salads.

• Green Beans: The deep green color of these beans will be enhanced when beans are sautéed in a hot fat.

• Julienne: cut with a knife or food processor into slices ¼-inch thick, then cut these slices into strips 1-inch long.

• Legumes: If there is not enough time to soak legumes, a quick way to tenderize them is too cover them with cold water. Bring legumes and water to a boil and for 2 minutes. Remove from heat and let stand, tightly covered, for 1 hour. An even faster way is to blanch the legumes for 2 minutes. This equals 8 hours of soaking.

• Potatoes: Cut out all green areas and eyes from potatoes, as they will give the potato dish a bitter taste.

• Soup Greens: When soup greens are specified in a recipe, use a piece of celeriac, parsnip, eek and carrot.

Preparing Vegetables

Blanching

Blanching means briefly precooking a vegetable, or cooking it in boiling salted water or in water to which lemon juice has been added. Single leaves of leafy vegetables are fully cooked by blanching. Whole leaves become easier to handle after blanching. The length of blanching time is measured from the time the blanching liquid returns to a boil. Blanch a portion at a time when preparing a large quantity of vegetables.

To prepare cooked cabbage salad or coleslaw, remove outer leaves, quarter the head, cut out the core and grate, shred or thinly slice.

Stir-frying

This method quick fries finely cut vegetables in a small amount of hot vegetable oil. Cut the vegetables into small, uniform pieces as called for in the recipe. Vegetables can be coated in flour or in bread crumbs. Reduce the heat after adding the vegetables and sauté, turning constantly. Serve breaded vegetables with a piquant sauce.

Dry trimmed and washed vegetables. Cut the vegetables into julienne strips. Heat a preferred cooking oil in a wok or large frying pan. Garlic, ginger and onions add a zesty taste to the stir-fried vegetables.

Steaming

Steaming is cooking in a sieve insert over steaming water, wine or herb liquid in a pan with a tight-fitting lid. The vegetables should not touch the water. Since nutrients from the steamed vegetables are contained in the cooking liquid, the liquid can be used later to prepare a sauce or soup.

To steam cauliflower, place about 1 inch of water in a saucepan and bring to a boil. Do not add salt when steaming cauliflower, since salt causes the white florets to discolor.

Simmering

Simmering is cooking over low heat with a small amount of liquid. The liquid may be derived from the vegetable itself, as with leaf vegetables, mushrooms, tomatoes, zucchini or onions. Avoid opening the saucepan when simmering a vegetable. Stir by shaking the pan. If necessary, additional liquid may be added when simmering larger quantities of vegetables.

To prepare tasty, fresh green beans, sauté diced onion and garlic with green beans in a large saucepan for 3 minutes, turning constantly.

Place ample water and some salt in a large saucepan and bring to a boil. Place the shredded cabbage in a sieve and immerse in the boiling water. Blanch for 5 minutes after the water returns to a boil.

Briefly drain the cabbage. Dip the sieve in a bowl of ice water, then drain well, squeezing out excess water if necessary. Continue preparing as described in the recipe.

Stir-fry thinly sliced portions of these for a few minutes before adding other vegetables to the oil.

Add the remaining vegetables and stir-fry for 6 to 10 minutes. Season the vegetables as indicated in the recipe and transfer to a serving dish.

Place the cauliflower head up in the steamer. Be sure the pan lid fits tightly. Steam cauliflower for 20 to 20 to 25 minutes. Other steaming times are given in recipes.

Transfer the cauliflower to a warm oven. Use the cooking liquid to prepare a cream sauce and pour over the cauliflower. Sprinkle with buttered, browned bread crumbs. Follow the recipe instructions for other steamed vegetables.

Add a little hot vegetable stock and simmer the beans, covered, for 10 to 15 minutes. Shake the covered pan to stir the beans.

Check once or twice to see if there is enough liquid in the pan, adding additional stock if necessary. Serve the beans sprinkled with fresh, chopped herbs.

Preparing Vegetables

Au Gratin

An au gratin dish refers to a layer of cheese, bread crumbs, crushed cornflakes, cracker crumbs, or finely ground nuts placed on top of a scalloped or sauced dish. The topping is browned in the oven or broiler to form a golden crust.

For potatoes au gratin, slice potatoes thinly. Arrange in layers in a greased, ovenproof pan. Season each layer with salt and pepper.

Broiling and Grilling

These cooking procedures use intense radiating heat over a grill, under a broiler or in a special grill frying pan. In broiling and grilling, only one side of the food at a time is exposed to the heating source. Brush the vegetable with seasoned oil. Broil or grill delicate vegetables on oiled aluminum foil. Vegetables to be grilled over charcoal should always be wrapped in an aluminum foil package.

To pan-grill eggplant, halve unpeeled eggplant lengthwise and sprinkle the cut surfaces with lemon juice.

Boiling

Boiling is a cooking method that uses a generous quantity of boiling water. Rapidly boiling or gently boiling water is used depending on the firmness of the vegetable. Use an uncovered saucepan if the liquid will be used to make a sauce, as this will allow some of the liquid to evaporate. The cooking liquid can be saved to prepare soup if it is not needed for a sauce, since this liquid is filled with nutrients from the cooked vegetable.

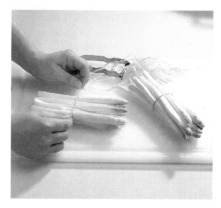

To cook asparagus, tie peeled asparagus into bundles of 10. Place water to cover, salt to taste, a pinch of sugar and some oil in a saucepan and bring to a boil.

Stewing

Stewing involves sautéeing the vegetable in a small amount of fat, then adding about 1 inch of boiling liquid around the vegetable. It is then cooked in a covered saucepan or stew pot. The heat is turned higher to bring the liquid to a boil, then lowered to a simmer. The stewing liquid is used in the sauce; it can be thickened with cream, wine and spices.

To make stuffed cabbage, cut the center rib of 2 or 3 cabbage leaves so that they lie flat. Lay the leaves one on top of the other, place desired filling in the middle, fold in the sides of the leaves and roll up.

Whisk egg and cream together, pour over the potatoes, sprinkle generously with grated Gruyère cheese and dot with butter.

Bake in a preheated 450°F oven for 30 to 40 minutes. Cover with aluminum foil if top begins to brown too quickly.

Place each eggplant half on a sufficiently large piece of aluminum foil. Generously brush with a preferred marinade and wrap the vegetable in the foil. Refrigerate for 1½ to 2 hours.

Place the eggplant halves in their foil packages, cut side down, in a grill frying pan and fry for 8 minutes. Turn and fry 8 minutes more. Reduce heat in pan. Open the foil, place the eggplant directly in the pan and brown briefly.

Place the asparagus in the boiling water. Adjust the heat to keep the water at a low boil. Cook, covered, for 15 to 20 minutes, depending on the thickness of the spears.

Check tenderness by piercing with a fork. The asparagus is done when it is easily pierced. Remove the bundles with a slotted spoon and drain.

Tie the rolls with string to keep them from opening up during the cooking process. Heat about 2 tablespoons of vegetable oil in a stew pot or a very large frying pan with lid.

Sauté the rolls on all sides in the hot oil until light brown. Pour in a hot stock and cook, tightly covered, for about 30 minutes.

Soups, Appetizers and Snacks

Sorrel Soup

215 calories per serving
Preparation time: 10 minutes
Cooking time: 25 minutes

| 3 green onions |
| 1 lb. potatoes |
| 3 cups vegetable stock |
| 1 tbs. vegetable oil |
| ½ lb. sorrel leaves |
| 1 large kohlrabi |
| ¼ cup chopped chervil |
| ⅛ tsp. salt |
| ⅛ tsp. white pepper |
| ¼ cup whipping cream |
| 1 egg yolk |

Trim green onions. Wash, dry and cut into thin rings. Peel, wash and dice potatoes. • Heat vegetable stock in a saucepan. •

Heat vegetable oil in a large saucepan and sauté onions until transparent. Add potatoes and hot stock and bring to a boil. Cover and simmer for 20 minutes. • Wash sorrel leaves. Drain well and chop coarsely. • Peel kohlrabi. Wash the tender green leaves, drain and chop finely. Combine chopped kohlrabi leaves and chervil; set aside for garnish. Grate peeled kohlrabi. • Add sorrel and grated kohlrabi to potatoes after 20 minutes and simmer 5 minutes longer. Season with salt and pepper. • Whisk whipping cream and egg yolk together. • To serve, remove soup from heat and stir in cream mixture. Garnish with chervil and kohlrabi leaves.

Cream of Corn Soup

210 calories per serving
Preparation time: 30 minutes
Cooking time: 5 minutes

| 1 lb. unshelled baby peas |
| ½ tsp. salt |
| 4 cups water |
| 1 14-oz. can corn |
| 2 tsp. cornstarch |
| 1 tsp. paprika |
| ¼ cup sour cream |
| ¼ cup chopped chives |

Shell peas, reserving pods. Wash and drain pods and place in a large saucepan with water and salt. Bring to a boil. Cover tightly and simmer for 20 minutes. Remove from heat and strain, reserving cooking liquid and discarding pods. • Puree corn and corn liquid in a blender or food processor. • Place reserved pod liquid in a saucepan and bring to a boil. Add peas and simmer for 5 minutes. Add pureed corn and additional water, if necessary. Bring to a boil, then reduce heat to low. • Stir cornstarch, paprika and a little cold water together until cornstarch is dissolved. Add mixture to soup, stirring constantly. • To serve, stir in sour cream and sprinkle with chopped chives.

Tip: Julienned green beans or green peppers can be substituted for peas. Replace water with vegetable stock.

Cream of Asparagus Soup

195 calories per serving
Preparation time: 15 minutes
Cooking time: 15 minutes

3⅓ lbs. green asparagus
½ tsp. salt
⅛ tsp. sugar
1 cup vegetable stock
⅛ tsp. white pepper
1 tbs. cornstarch
7 tbs. sour cream
2 tbs. chopped fresh dill

Wash, dry and thinly peel bottom part of asparagus spears. Cut off woody ends. Cut asparagus tips into 2-inch pieces and set aside. • Cut rest of asparagus spears into 1-inch pieces and place in a saucepan with salt, sugar and water to cover. Cook, covered, for 15 minutes. Remove from heat. • Place vegetable stock in a separate saucepan and bring to a boil. Add asparagus tips, cover and simmer for 8 minutes. • Puree asparagus pieces and their cooking liquid in a blender or food processor. • Drain asparagus tips, reserving cooking liquid. Place reserved cooking liquid and pureed asparagus in large saucepan and heat gently. Season with pepper and salt, if desired. • Stir cornstarch with a little cold water until cornstarch is dissolved. Add to soup, stirring constantly. Stir in sour cream. • To serve, add asparagus tips and cook until heated through. Garnish with chopped dill.

Tip: Garnish with thinly sliced smoked ham for a heartier soup.

Cream of Tomato Soup

200 calories per serving
Preparation time: 20 minutes
Cooking time: 15 minutes

3⅓ lbs. tomatoes	
2 onions	
1 clove garlic	
2 tbs. olive oil	
¼ tsp. salt	
⅛ tsp. black pepper	
½ tsp. paprika	
1 tbs. chopped, mixed fresh herbs, such as basil, oregano, thyme and rosemary	
½ tsp. sugar	
1 cup vegetable stock	
¼ cup sour cream	
¼ cup freshly grated Parmesan cheese	

Cut tomatoes into cubes. Peel and finely chop onions and garlic cloves. • Heat olive oil in a large saucepan. Add onions and garlic and sauté until transparent. Add diced tomatoes, salt, pepper, paprika, herbs and sugar. Simmer, covered, for 15 minutes, stirring frequently. • Heat vegetable stock in a separate saucepan. Add hot stock to tomato mixture. Remove from heat and puree in a blender or food processor. • Return puree to saucepan and bring to a boil. Immediately remove from heat and ladle into soup bowls. • To serve, spoon 1 tablespoon of sour cream on each serving and sprinkle with Parmesan cheese.

Tip: Use very ripe, meaty tomatoes for a flavorful soup.

Cucumber Soup

175 calories per serving
Preparation time: 10 minutes
Cooking time: 20 minutes

2¼ lbs. cucumbers	
1 tsp. fresh, or ½ tsp. dried, rosemary	
2 cups vegetable stock	
1 to 2 tsp. lemon juice	
1 tsp. maple syrup	
⅛ tsp. salt	
⅛ tsp. white pepper	
⅔ cup sour cream	
6 tbs. finely chopped fresh dill	

Cut an 8-inch long piece from one cucumber and set aside. • Thinly peel remaining cucumbers. Cut in half lengthwise, scrape out seeds with a teaspoon and cut pulp into 1-inch cubes. • Place cucumber cubes, rosemary and vegetable stock in a large saucepan and bring to a boil. Cover and simmer for 20 minutes. • Wash, dry and cube reserved unpeeled piece of cucumber. • To serve, stir cubed cucumber, lemon juice, maple syrup, salt, pepper and sour cream into soup. Sprinkle with dill.

Tip: Freshly grated horseradish can be used instead of rosemary to season soup.

Zucchini Soup

(left photograph)

280 calories per serving
Preparation time: 25 minutes
Cooking time: 20 minutes

1 ⅔ lbs. zucchini
4 shallots
¼ cup corn oil
3 cups hot poultry stock
½ tsp. salt
2 tsp. paprika
⅔ lb. chicken breasts
¼ cup whipping cream
2 tsp. finely chopped sage

Thinly peel and about 1 lb. of the zucchini. Wash and dry remainder and set aside. Peel and dice shallots. • Heat ⅛ cup corn oil in a large saucepan. Add shallots and sauté until transparent.

Add diced zucchini and poultry stock and bring to a boil. Cover and simmer for 15 minutes. Strain and season with salt and paprika. Return to saucepan. • Cut reserved zucchini into pieces 2 to 3 inches long and ⅛ inch thick. Add to the soup and simmer for 5 minutes. • Cut chicken breasts into cubes. • Heat remaining oil in a frying pan. Add chicken cubes and stir-fry for 5 minutes. Add chicken to soup. • To serve, stir in whipping cream and sprinkle with sage.

Cauliflower Soup

(right photograph)

220 calories per serving
Preparation time: 30 minutes
Cooking time: 25 minutes

1 cauliflower (about 2¼ lbs.)
½ lb. leeks
1 onion
2 tbs. safflower oil
1 tbs. flour
⅛ tsp. cayenne
1 tsp. salt
1 tbs. margarine
¼ cup sunflower seeds
¼ cup chopped dandelion leaves

Remove leaves from cauliflower and trim stem. Place in a saucepan, cover with water, and simmer for 25 minutes.

Drain, reserving cooking liquid. Divide cauliflower into florets and dice stem; set aside. • Trim root end and dark green leaves from leeks. Wash white parts and slice into thin rings. Peel and dice onion. • Heat safflower oil in a large saucepan. Add onion and sauté until transparent, stirring constantly. Add leek and sauté for 3 minutes. Add flour and sauté briefly. Slowly pour 4 cups of cauliflower cooking liquid into onion and leek mixture. Bring to a boil. Season with cayenne and salt. • Add reserved cauliflower florets and diced stems. Cook over low heat until heated through. • Melt margarine in a frying pan. Add sunflower seeds and sauté until golden brown. To serve, sprinkle sunflower seeds and chopped dandelion leaves over soup.

Kohlrabi Soup

95 calories per serving without meatballs
320 calories per serving with meatballs
Preparation time: 10 minutes
Cooking time: 30 minutes

For the soup:
2¼ lbs. kohlrabi
3 cups vegetable stock
⅛ tsp. salt
⅛ tsp. white pepper
For the meat balls:
¼ lb. ground beef
¼ lb. ground pork
1 egg
⅓ cup bread crumbs
⅛ tsp. salt
⅛ tsp. white pepper
⅛ tsp. dried marjoram
¼ cup mixed herbs such as lovage and fennel

Peel the kohlrabi, reserving the tender leaves. Cut the kohlrabi into julienne strips. • Place julienned kohlrabi, vegetable stock, and seasonings in a large saucepan and bring to a boil. Cover and cook over medium heat for 20 minutes. • For the meatballs, combine ground beef and pork, egg, bread crumbs, salt, white pepper and marjoram. Mix until well blended. Shape into walnut-sized balls. • Add meatballs to the soup and simmer, uncovered, for 8 to 10 minutes. • Combine herbs and reserved kohlrabi leaves; wash, dry and chop finely. • To serve, ladle soup and meatballs into serving bowls. Sprinkle finely chopped herbs and kohlrabi leaves over soup.

Fennel Soup

270 calories per serving
Preparation time: 10 minutes
Cooking time: 25 minutes

2¼ lbs. fennel
⅔ lb. potatoes
1 large onion
3 cloves garlic
1 bay leaf
1 tsp. salt
4 cups water
2 large, tart apples
1 tbs. butter
3 tbs. chopped parsley

Trim, wash and cut fennel into small pieces, reserving the tender fennel stalks and leaves.

Peel and dice potatoes, onion and garlic cloves. • Place prepared ingredients, bay leaf, salt and water in a large saucepan. Bring to a boil. Cover and simmer for 25 minutes. • Peel and coarsely grate apples. Wash, dry and finely chop reserved fennel stalks and leaves. • Remove soup from heat and strain. Return to saucepan and stir in grated apples. Simmer until heated through. • To serve, melt butter in a frying pan. Briefly stir-fry chopped parsley and finely chopped fennel greens. Sprinkle stir-fried greens over soup.

Tip: Leek soup can be prepared following the above recipe, substituting leeks for the fennel. Omit grated apples and sprinkle prepared soup with croutons and chopped chives.

Strained Carrot Soup

230 calories per serving
Preparation time: 15 minutes
Cooking time: 30 minutes

1⅔ lbs. carrots
3 cups vegetable stock
1 tbs. flour
3 tbs. butter
⅛ tsp. salt
⅛ tsp. white pepper
4 drops of lemon juice
⅛ tsp. sugar
2 slices whole-wheat bread
3 tbs. whipping cream
2 tbs. chopped fresh herbs such as dill, parsley or chives

Scrape, wash and cut carrots into small cubes. • Place carrots and vegetable stock in a saucepan and bring to a boil. Cover and simmer over low heat for 30 minutes. • Puree carrots and their cooking liquid in a blender or food processor. Return to saucepan. • Mix flour and 2 tablespoons of butter. Whisk into soup until flour is dissolved. Simmer soup over low heat for a few minutes. Season with salt, pepper, lemon juice and sugar. • Cut bread into ½-inch cubes. Melt remaining butter in a frying pan. Add bread cubes and sauté until golden brown. • To serve, stir whipping cream into soup. Garnish with croutons and chopped herbs.

Minestrone

270 calories per serving
Serves: 8
Soaking time: 12 hours
Preparation time: 20 minutes
Cooking time: 1 hour, 30 minutes

½ cup navy beans	
¼ lb. celery	
¼ lb. potatoes	
⅓ lb. zucchini	
¼ lb. carrots	
¼ lb. leek	
¼ lb. unshelled green peas	
¼ cup olive oil	
6 cups poultry stock	
1 bay leaf	
½ cup parsley	
1 small onion	

1 clove garlic
6 strips bacon
4 tomatoes
1 cup cooked rice
1 tsp. salt
⅛ tsp. black pepper
1 tbs. chopped fresh basil
½ cup freshly grated Parmesan cheese

Wash and sort navy beans. Soak beans in cold water to cover for 12 hours. • Place beans and soaking water in a large saucepan and bring to a boil. Cover and simmer for 1 hour. • Cut celery into slices. Peel and dice potatoes. Slice zucchini. Scrape and dice carrots. Thoroughly wash leek and slice into rings. Shell peas. Combine peas with celery, potatoes, zucchini, carrots and leeks. • Heat olive oil in a large saucepan or stock pot. Add vegetables and stir-fry for 3 minutes. Remove pan from heat and set aside. • Heat poultry stock in a separate saucepan. Tie bay leaf and parsley. Add hot stock, parsley bouquet, beans and their cooking liquid to the vegetables. Simmer, covered, for 30 minutes. • Peel and finely dice onion and garlic clove. Dice bacon and sauté in a dry pan until crisp. Remove bacon from pan with a slotted spoon and set aside. Add diced onion and garlic and sauté in bacon fat until golden. • Peel and dice tomatoes. • Add diced tomatoes, cooked rice, bacon, onion and garlic to the soup. Season with salt and pepper. • To serve, sprinkle with chopped basil and grated Parmesan cheese.

Pureed Potato Soup
(left photograph)

350 calories per serving
Preparation time: 15 minutes
Cooking time: 20 minutes

1 lb. potatoes
½ tsp. salt
1 to 2 cups meat stock
⅔ lb. trimmed, white leek pieces
6 strips lb. bacon
1 large onion
7 tbs. whipping cream
2 tbs. chopped parsley

Peel and dice potatoes. Place in a saucepan with salt and water to cover. Bring to a boil. Cover and simmer for 20 minutes.

• Thoroughly wash leek and cut into rings. Place leek, and a little water in a separate saucepan. Bring to a boil. Cover and simmer for 15 minutes. • Dice bacon. Peel and slice onion into rings. • Puree cooked potatoes and their liquid in a blender or food processor. Stir leek rings and their cooking liquid into puree. Add hot meat stock until soup is smooth. Stir in whipping cream. • Sauté bacon in a dry pan until crisp. Remove bacon from pan and drain. Add onion rings and sauté in bacon fat until golden. Remove from pan with a slotted spoon. • To serve, sprinkle parsley, bacon and onion rings over soup.

Potato Soup with Watercress
(right photograph)

235 calories per serving
Preparation time: 10 minutes
Cooking time: 15 to 20 minutes

1½ lbs. potatoes
⅔ lb. carrots
3 cups vegetable stock
2 shallots
1 clove garlic
⅔ lb. watercress
2 tbs. vegetable oil
⅛ tsp. salt
⅛ tsp. cayenne

Peel and dice potatoes. Scrape and dice carrots. • Place diced potatoes, carrots and vegetable stock in a large saucepan and bring to a boil. Simmer for 15 to 20 minutes, or until vegetables are tender. • Peel and finely dice the shallots and garlic clove. Coarsely chop watercress. Set one-third of the watercress aside. • Heat vegetable oil in a frying pan. Add shallots and garlic and sauté until golden. Add two-thirds of the watercress and stir-fry for 5 minutes. • Stir watercress mixture into soup. Season with salt and cayenne. To serve, garnish with reserved watercress.

Navy Bean Soup

435 calories per serving
Soaking time: 12 hours
Preparation time: 10 minutes
Cooking time: 1 hour, 45 minutes

1 cup navy beans	
5 cups cold water	
1 bunch of soup greens	
1 large potato	
1 large onion	
1 large carrot	
1 green pepper	
1 red pepper	
½ tsp. salt	
½ tsp. paprika	
⅛ tsp. white pepper	
⅛ tsp. cayenne	
2 large tomatoes	
6 strips bacon	
2 tbs. chopped parsley	

Wash and sort navy beans. Soak beans in cold water for 12 hours. • Place beans and soaking water in a large saucepan and bring to a boil, skimming any scum that rises to the surface. • Trim and coarsely chop soup greens and add to beans. Cover and simmer for 1½ hours. • Peel and dice potato, onion and carrot. Remove inner membrane and seeds from peppers and cut into julienne strips. • Add potato, onion, carrot and peppers to beans. Simmer 15 minutes longer. Season with salt, paprika, white pepper and cayenne. • Peel and dice tomatoes, then add to soup. Dice bacon and sauté in a dry pan until crisp. Remove bacon from pan, drain and add to soup. • To serve, garnish soup with chopped parsley.

Lentil Soup

365 calories per serving
Preparation time: 5 minutes
Cooking time: 1 hour, 30 minutes

1½ cups lentils	
4 cups water	
1 large carrot	
1 onion	
⅛ lb. celeriac	
2 large potatoes	
1 tsp. salt	
⅛ tsp. black pepper	
½ cup dry red wine	

Wash and sort lentils. Place lentils and water in a large saucepan and bring to a boil. Cover and simmer for 1 to 1½ hours, or until lentils are tender.

Frequently skim scum that rises to the surface during the first 15 minutes. • Scrape and dice carrots. Peel and dice onion, celeriac and potatoes. • Add vegetables to cooked lentils and simmer 20 minutes longer. Season with salt and pepper. • To serve, remove soup from heat and stir in red wine.

Tip: The lentils can be cooked in 2 cups of red wine and 2 cups of water. Half a cup of red wine should still be mixed into the finished soup. For a heartier soup, add diced, smoked sausages.

Leek Soup

300 calories per serving
Preparation time: 40 minutes
Cooking time: 20 minutes

For the soup:
1⅓ lbs. leek
2 tbs. vegetable oil
⅓ lb. shelled peas
4 cups hot vegetable stock
⅛ tsp. nutmeg
⅛ tsp. salt
⅛ tsp. white pepper
For the cheese dumplings:
3 tbs. margarine
1 egg
⅓ to ½ cup whole-wheat semolina
½ cup freshly grated Emmenthaler cheese
⅛ tsp. grated lemon rind
⅛ tsp. salt
⅛ tsp. white pepper
2 tbs. chopped chives

Trim hard green leaves and root end from leeks. Cut white part in half lengthwise, then slice thinly. • Heat vegetable oil in a large saucepan or stock pot. Add leek slices and sauté for 3 minutes. Add peas and vegetable stock. Bring to a boil. Cover and simmer for 20 minutes. • Cream margarine and egg together. Mix in semolina, grated cheese, lemon rind, salt and pepper. Set mixture aside for 20 minutes. • Place water and salt in another saucepan and bring to a boil. Cut dumplings from semolina mixture with a wet teaspoon. Cook dumplings in simmering water for 10 to 15 minutes. • To serve, season soup with nutmeg, salt and pepper. Place dumplings in the soup and garnish with chopped chives.

Waldorf Salad

435 calories per serving
Preparation time: 15 minutes
Refrigeration time: 1 hour

⅔ lb. celeriac
½ lb. slightly tart apples
2 tbs. lemon juice
½ tsp. salt
½ cup walnuts
⅔ cup mayonnaise
½ cup whipping cream
½ to 1 tsp. sugar

Peel, wash and dry celeriac. Cut celeriac into julienne strips. Peel, core and cut apples into julienne strips. Combine celeriac and apples and sprinkle with lemon juice. Add salt and refrigerate for 1 hour. • Chop walnuts and combine with mayonnaise, whipping cream and sugar. • To serve, fold mayonnaise mixture into apples and celeriac.

Broiled Eggplant

205 calories per serving
Refrigeration time: 1½ hours
Cooking time: 25 minutes

| 2 medium-sized eggplants |
| 1 tbs. lemon juice |
| 3 cloves garlic |
| 2 tbs. green peppercorns |
| 6 tbs. olive oil |
| 2 tbs. fresh thyme leaves |
| 1 tsp. salt |
| ⅛ tsp. black pepper |

Wash and dry eggplants. Cut off stems and halve eggplants lengthwise. Brush lemon juice onto cut surfaces. • Peel and finely chop garlic cloves. Finely chop green peppercorns. Combine olive oil, chopped garlic, green peppercorns, thyme, salt and black pepper. • Place each eggplant half, cut side up, on a large piece of aluminum foil. Score cut surfaces with a fork and generously sprinkle with olive oil mixture. Wrap eggplant halves in the aluminum foil and refrigerate for 1½ hours. • Preheat oven to 450°F. • Place eggplants in the foil, cut side down, in oven and bake for 10 minutes. Open foil packet, turn eggplant over and bake, cut side up, for 15 minutes. • Sprinkle eggplant halves with remaining oil and serve.

Baked Tomatoes with Mozzarella Cheese

405 calories per serving
Preparation time: 10 minutes
Cooking time: 25 minutes

| Olive oil for greasing |
| 4 large tomatoes (about 1¾ lbs.) |
| ⅔ lb. Mozzarella cheese |
| 2 medium-sized onions |
| 2 cloves garlic |
| ½ tsp. salt |
| 2 tbs. olive oil |
| ⅛ tsp. white pepper |
| 1 tbs. fresh thyme |

Preheat oven to 425°F. • Grease an ovenproof dish with olive oil. • Cut tomatoes and cheese into ½-inch thick slices. Place cheese and tomato slices in ovenproof dish in alternating layers. • Peel and finely dice onions and garlic cloves. Sprinkle salt over diced garlic and crush with a fork. Combine olive oil, diced onions, garlic and pepper and sprinkle over tomato and cheese slices. • Place dish on middle rack of oven and bake for 20 minutes. • Wash and dry thyme and sprinkle over the dish. Bake 5 minutes longer. Serve hot or cold.

Broiled Avocados

325 calories per serving
Preparation time: 10 minutes
Baking time: 10 to 15 minutes

2 firm avocados	
2 tsp. lemon juice	
12 anchovy fillets	
2 tbs. small capers	
½ onion, peeled	
⅛ tsp. of Tabasco sauce	
1 tbs. walnut oil	
¼ tbs. sour cream	
2 slices of cheese	

Preheat oven to 450°F. • Cut avocados in half and remove seeds. Scoop out two-thirds of the flesh and dice finely. Sprinkle the diced avocado and avocado shells with lemon juice. • Dice anchovies, capers and peeled onions.

Stir together with diced avocado, Tabasco sauce, walnut oil and sour cream. • Cut a thin slice from the bottom of each avocado shell so it stands firmly. Fill avocado halves with diced avocado mixture and place on oven rack. Dice cheese slices and sprinkle over avocados. • Bake until cheese melts and a golden brown crust forms.

Tip: Two chopped herring fillets and a dill pickle can be substituted for anchovies and capers in the filling.

Fennel with Aïoli Sauce

745 calories per serving
Preparation time: 20 minutes

4 medium-sized fennel bulbs (about 1¾ lbs.)	
2 tsp. lemon juice	
1 slice white bread with crust removed	
½ cup milk	
6 cloves garlic	
2 egg yolks	
1 cup olive oil	
1 to 2 tsp. tarragon vinegar	
½ tsp. salt	
⅛ tsp. white pepper	

Trim tender green leaves and stalks from fennel bulbs. Wash, dry, and finely chop tender greens. Cover and set aside. •

Remove hard layers from fennel bulbs, then cut bulbs into julienne strips. Sprinkle with lemon juice, cover and set aside. • Soak bread in milk. Peel garlic cloves and squeeze through a garlic press. Squeeze out bread well. Combine bread, egg yolks and crushed garlic and blend well. Add olive oil to the garlic mixture a drop at a time at first, then a teaspoon at a time. Blend until mixture has the consistency of mayonnaise. Season with tarragon vinegar, salt and pepper. Sprinkle with chopped fennel greens. Transfer sauce to a small serving bowl. • To serve, place fennel julienne on salad plates and serve Aïoli sauce on the side.

Stuffed Artichokes

350 calories per serving
Preparation time: 10 minutes
Baking time: 50 to 60 minutes

| 6 cups water |
| 2 tsp. salt |
| 1 tbs. lemon juice |
| 4 artichokes |
| 1 small onion |
| 1 clove garlic |
| ¼ lb. mushrooms |
| ½ lb. shrimp, peeled and deveined |
| ½ cup milk |
| 1 tbs. olive oil |
| 1 tbs. flour |
| ½ cup whipping cream |
| ⅛ tsp. white pepper |
| ⅔ cup freshly grated Gruyère cheese |
| 2 tbs. butter |
| Oil for greasing |

Place water, salt and lemon juice in a large saucepan and bring to a boil. • Trim artichoke stems and remove hard outer leaves. Cut tips off remaining leaves. Place stem side down in the boiling water and boil gently, uncovered, for 30 minutes. • Remove artichokes from water with a slotted spoon, drain and set aside to cool. • Preheat oven to 400°F. • Peel and finely chop onion and garlic clove. Clean and chop mushrooms. Rinse shrimp with cold water, drain and dice. • Heat milk. • Heat olive oil in a saucepan. Add onions and garlic and sauté until golden, stirring constantly. Add flour and sauté briefly. Slowly pour in warm milk. Simmer for 5 minutes, stirring constantly. • Add whipping cream, white pepper, chopped mushrooms and shrimp. • Grease an ovenproof dish with olive oil. •

Push artichoke leaves apart and remove fuzzy center. Place filling in middle of artichokes and between outer leaves. Arrange artichokes in ovenproof dish. Sprinkle with grated cheese and dot with butter. • Bake for 20 to 30 minutes, until cheese is melted and artichokes are lightly browned.

Stuffed Tomatoes

270 calories per serving
8 Servings
Preparation time: 10 minutes

| 8 medium-sized tomatoes |
| 1 tsp. salt |
| ¾ cup cooked rice |
| 7 ozs. tuna fish |
| 2 tbs. chopped parsley |
| ⅛ tsp. black pepper |
| ½ tsp. grated lemon rind |
| ¼ cup sour cream |
| 8 small fresh basil leaves |

Wash and dry tomatoes. Cut a thin slice off of the stemless ends and set aside to use as tops. Hollow out pulp with a sharp-edged teaspoon. Sprinkle inside of tomatoes with salt. • Put rice in a bowl. Drain tuna, separate into flakes and stir into rice. Add parsley, pepper, grated lemon rind and sour cream. Mix gently. • Spoon tuna mixture into tomatoes and cover with reserved tomato tops. • To serve, wash and dry basil leaves. Garnish each tomato with 1 basil leaf.

Tip: A rice and bean sprout mixture can be substituted for the rice and tuna mixture; omit lemon rind.

Toasted Swiss Chard Sandwich

250 calories per serving
Preparation time: 10 minutes
Baking time: 15 minutes

1 lb. Swiss chard
2 cups water
½ tsp. salt
4 slices white bread, toasted
2 tbs. butter
2 eggs
¼ cup sour cream
½ cup freshly grated Emmenthaler cheese

Remove stalks and middle ribs from Swiss chard. Wash and drain leaves. • Bring water and salt to a boil in a large saucepan. Add Swiss chard and cook, covered, over low heat for 5 minutes.

Drain and cut into julienne strips. • Preheat oven to 450°F. • Thinly spread bread slices with 1 tablespoon of butter. • Whisk eggs and sour cream. Melt remaining butter in a frying pan. Add egg mixture, turning constantly with a wooden spoon until eggs have thickened but are still soft. • Divide Swiss chard among 4 slices of toast. Spoon egg mixture on top and sprinkle with grated cheese. • Place bread slices on a cookie sheet and bake on upper rack of oven for 10 minutes, or until cheese has a golden crust.

Tip: Spinach can be substituted for the Swiss chard. Blanch 1 lb. spinach in 4 cups of boiling, salted water for 1 minute. Drain well and place on buttered toast. Proceed with recipe at this point.

Asparagus Sandwiches

355 calories per serving
Preparation time: 15 minutes
Cooking time: 30 minutes

2¼ lbs. white asparagus
1 tsp. salt
1 tsp. sugar
8 cups water
4 slices of white bread
2 tbs. softened butter
½ lb. cooked shrimp, peeled and deveined
¼ cup sour cream
¼ cup freshly grated Swiss cheese
2 tbs. chopped fresh dill

Thinly peel asparagus spears from top to bottom and break off woody ends. Tie asparagus

into 3 bunches. • Place salt, sugar and water in a large saucepan and bring to a boil. • Add asparagus and simmer, covered, for 10 to 15 minutes, depending on thickness of asparagus. • Remove asparagus and cut off tips about 2 ½ inches long. Reserve remaining pieces and cooking liquid for soup. Drain asparagus tips. • Cut off bread crusts and butter the slices. • Preheat oven to 450°F. • Rinse shrimp with cold water and drain well. Divide asparagus tips among the 4 slices of bread and place shrimp on top. • Place sandwiches on a cookie sheet lined with aluminum foil. Combine sour cream and grated Swiss cheese and spread over shrimp. • Bake sandwiches until cheese melts. • Sprinkle with dill to serve.

Vegetables in Aspic

230 calories per serving
Preparation time: 30 minutes
Cooking time: 30 minutes
Refrigeration time: 5 to 6 hours

1 cup water
½ tsp. salt
8 white peppercorns
2 bunches mixed herbs, such as celery leaves, parsley, chervil and tarragon
1 small cauliflower (about 1 lb.)
½ lb. shelled peas
½ cup fresh dill
2 cups parsley leaves
3 sprigs peppermint
2 envelopes unflavored gelatin
2 cups white wine
⅛ tsp. white pepper
⅛ tsp. sugar
1 tsp. lemon juice
2 hard-boiled eggs

Place water, salt and white peppercorns in a saucepan and bring to a boil. Add mixed herbs. Cover and cook over low heat for 10 minutes. • Strain herb stock into another saucepan. • Divide cauliflower into florets, wash thoroughly and trim stems. • Bring herb stock to a boil. Add cauliflower florets, cover pan and simmer for 20 minutes. • Remove florets with a slotted spoon and plunge into ice water. Spread florets on a paper towel to cool. • Bring herb stock back to a boil. Add peas and cook in gently boiling stock for 10 minutes. • Remove peas with a slotted spoon, plunge into ice water and drain on a paper towel. • Wash and dry dill, parsley and peppermint. Set aside. • Dissolve gelatin according to package directions. Pour into herb stock and add white wine and enough water to make 3 cups of liquid. Season with salt to taste, white pepper, sugar and lemon juice. Cool. • Rinse a large mold with cold water and pour in ¼ inch of gelatin liquid. Refrigerate until set. • Peel and slice eggs. Place egg slices on the jelled surface. Place a few dill leaves between eggs. Pour a thin layer of gelatin liquid over eggs and refrigerate until set. • Arrange half of the peas on jelled surface and cover with cauliflower florets. Pour a thin layer of gelatin liquid on top and refrigerate until set. • Arrange parsley leaves on top of cauliflower, reserving a few for garnish. Cover with remaining peas and pour remaining gelatin liquid on top. Refrigerate for 3 to 4 hours, or until set. • To serve, loosen gelatin from mold with a sharp knife. Dip mold briefly into hot water, then turn gelatin out onto a serving platter. • Garnish with reserved parsley, dill and peppermint.

Spinach Soufflé

385 calories per serving
Preparation time: 1 hour
Cooking time: 25 minutes

2¼ lbs. fresh spinach
4 cups water
1½ tsp. salt
6 shallots
½ cup parsley
2 tbs. vegetable oil
2 tsp. lemon juice
½ cup milk
3 tbs. butter
¼ cup flour
⅛ tsp. cayenne
⅛ tsp. nutmeg
½ cup grated Parmesan cheese
4 eggs, separated
⅛ tsp. black pepper
Butter for greasing

Wash spinach. • Place water and 1 teaspoon of salt in a saucepan and bring to a boil. Add spinach and cook for 1 minute; drain. • Peel and finely chop shallots. Chop parsley. • Heat vegetable oil in a large saucepan. Add shallots and sauté until transparent. Add spinach, parsley and lemon juice and sauté for 1 minute. Remove from heat. • Heat milk in a small saucepan. Add butter and flour and bring to a boil, stirring constantly. Season with cayenne and nutmeg. • Remove from heat and stir in Parmesan cheese. Slowly fold egg yolks into sauce. Stir in spinach and season with salt to taste and black pepper. • Preheat oven to 350°F. Grease 4 custard cups or ramekins with butter. • Beat egg whites until stiff and fold into spinach mixture. • Fill custard cups two-thirds full with spinach mixture and bake on middle rack of oven for 25 minutes. • Serve immediately.

Broccoli Soufflé

235 calories per serving
Preparation time: 45 minutes
Cooking time: 40 minutes

1 ¾ lbs. broccoli
8 cups water
1 tsp. salt
2 tbs. cornstarch
¼ cup sour cream
3 eggs, separated
½ cup freshly grated Parmesan cheese
Butter for greasing

Trim broccoli. Divide into florets and cut stalks into pieces. Place water and salt in a saucepan and bring to a boil. Add broccoli, cover and simmer for 10 minutes. Drain broccoli, reserving cooking liquid. • Combine cornstarch and sour cream. Puree broccoli, a portion at a time, in a blender or food processor, adding 1 to 2 tablespoons of cooking liquid to each portion. Return puree to saucepan and add cornstarch mixture. Bring to a boil, stirring constantly. Reduce heat to low. • Stir egg yolks and salt to taste into broccoli puree. • Preheat oven 400°F. • Beat egg whites until stiff and fold into broccoli puree with Parmesan cheese. • Grease bottom and sides of a 7-inch soufflé dish with butter. Pour in the broccoli mixture and bake on middle oven rack for 40 minutes. • Serve immediately.

Marinated Green Beans

490 calories per serving
Serves: 8
Preparation time: 1 hour
Cooking time: 20 minutes
Refrigeration time: 3 days

4½ lbs. young green beans
16 cups water
1 tbs. salt
1 cup fresh summer savory
3 cups sugar
3 cloves
2 tsp. turmeric
3 cups white wine vinegar

Trim and wash beans. • Place water, salt and summer savory in a large saucepan and bring to a boil. Add beans, cover pan and simmer for 15 minutes. • Drain beans, reserving 1 cup of cooking liquid and discarding summer savory. • Place reserved cooking liquid in a saucepan. Add sugar, cloves and turmeric. Simmer over low heat, stirring constantly, until sugar is completely dissolved. Pour vinegar into sugar mixture and bring to a boil. Reduce heat and simmer, uncovered, for 5 minutes. • Place beans in a large, glass oven-to-refrigerator container with a lid. Pour in hot vinegar liquid, close container and set aside until beans cool. Refrigerate. • Once a day, for the next 3 days, drain beans, reserving vinegar liquid. Place vinegar liquid in a saucepan and bring to a boil. Remove from heat and pour hot liquid over beans in glass oven-to-refrigerator container. Cool slightly, then return beans to the refrigerator. • After 3 days of marinating, beans can be held, covered, in the refrigerator for up to 4 weeks.

Marinated Peppers

400 calories per serving
Serves: 8
Preparation time: 40 minutes
Cooking time: 10 minutes
Refrigeration time: 3 days

3 yellow peppers
3 green peppers
3 red peppers
1 lb. shallots
2 cloves garlic
2 tsp. salt
1 tsp. dried oregano
3 cups cider vinegar
2 bay leaves
3 cups sugar
Water

Preheat oven to 500°F. • Place peppers on middle oven rack and bake until skins blister and burst. Cool peppers, then remove the skins. • Peel and quarter shallots. Peel and dice garlic cloves. Sprinkle garlic with salt and crush with a fork. Quarter peppers, remove inner membrane and seeds and chop. Place chopped peppers, shallots, garlic, oregano, vinegar, bay leaves and sugar in a saucepan. Fill with enough water to cover. Bring to a boil. • Reduce heat and simmer for 10 minutes. Remove from heat and transfer all ingredients to a large, oven-to-refrigerator container with a lid. Cover and refrigerate. • Once a day, for the next 3 days, drain peppers, reserving liquid. Place liquid in a saucepan and bring to a boil. Remove from heat and pour hot liquid over peppers in glass, oven-to-refrigerator container. Cover and refrigerate. • The marinated peppers can be stored in the refrigerator for up to 4 weeks.

Sweet and Sour Mixed Vegetables

470 calories per serving
Serves: 8
Preparation time: 30 minutes
Refrigeration time: 3 days

2¼ lbs. small, ripe tomatoes
1 lb. shallots
1 lb. okra
Juice and grated rind of 1 lemon
1 tbs. salt
4 white peppercorns
10 mustard seeds
3 cups sugar
3 cups apple vinegar

Peel and halve tomatoes, removing stem end. Peel and halve shallots. Wash and trim okra; cut in half lengthwise. Combine tomatoes, shallots and okra in a glass, oven-to-refrigerator bowl. • Place lemon juice, grated rind, salt, peppercorns, mustard seeds, sugar and vinegar in a saucepan. Cook over low heat until sugar is dissolved, stirring constantly. Pour liquid over vegetables, cover and marinate for 12 hours. • Strain vegetables, reserving liquid. Return vegetables to glass, oven- to-refrigerator bowl and place liquid in a saucepan. Bring to a boil, reduce heat and simmer for 5 minutes. Remove from heat and pour hot liquid over vegetables. Let vegetables cool. Refrigerate. • Once a day, for the next 2 days, repeat process of heating liquid and pouring it over vegetables. • The marinated vegetables are best after they have been refrigerated for 4 weeks. • Serve vegetables at room temperature.

Combination Dishes

Sorrel and Poached Eggs

225 calories per serving
Preparation and cooking time: 30 minutes

2 green onions	
1¾ ozs. young sorrel leaves	
⅔ lb. cucumber	
1 tbs. margarine	
⅛ tsp. salt	
1 tsp. honey	
1 tsp. mustard	
⅛ tsp. white pepper	
⅔ cup plain yogurt	
½ cup whipping cream	
2 tbs. chopped dill	
8 cups water	
1 tsp. salt	
2 tbs. vinegar	
4 eggs	

Trim, wash and chop green onions. Sort sorrel, removing tough stems; wash, dry and chop. Wash, dry and grate unpeeled cucumber. • Melt margarine in a saucepan. Add onions and sauté until transparent. Add sorrel and simmer for 5 minutes, stirring constantly. • Cool vegetables, then stir in grated cucumber, salt, honey, mustard and white pepper. Stir in yogurt. • Whip cream until stiff and fold into creamed sorrel. Sprinkle with dill. • Place water, salt and vinegar in a saucepan and bring to a boil. Break eggs into a cup and carefully slide into the boiling water. Return water to a boil. Immediately remove from heat and steep eggs in the hot water for 5 minutes. • Remove eggs with a slotted spoon, trim edges and arrange on serving platter. Serve with creamed sorrel.

Omelette with Wild Herbs

300 calories per serving
Preparation and cooking time: 40 minutes

⅓ lb. mixed wild herbs, such as young daisies, shepherd's purse, chervil, lime-tree leaves and dandelion	
2 shallots	
1 clove garlic	
½ tsp. salt	
3 tbs. vegetable oil	
⅛ tsp. salt	
⅛ tsp. white pepper	
8 eggs	
¼ cup whipping cream	
½ tsp. salt	
⅛ tsp. black pepper	

Wash, dry and chop herbs, removing thick stems. Peel and chop shallots. Peel garlic, cut into pieces, sprinkle with salt and crush with a fork. • Heat 1 tablespoon of vegetable oil in a frying pan. Add shallots and sauté until transparent. Add wild herbs and garlic and stir-fry for 5 minutes. Season with salt and pepper. • Whisk eggs, cream, salt and pepper together. Divide egg mixture into 4 portions. • Heat ½ tablespoon of vegetable oil in a frying pan. Add one portion of egg mixture to make an omelette. Stir eggs with the back of a spoon during first few minutes, then rotate pan gently until bottom of omelette is firm. Place one-quarter of the herbs on half the omelette. Fold omelette and slide onto a warmed plate. Transfer to a warm oven. Repeat procedure with remaining eggs to make 4 omelettes.

Asparagus with Cheese Sauce
(lower middle photograph)

310 calories per serving
Preparation time: 20 minutes
Cooking time: 25 to 35 minutes

3⅓ lbs. fresh, white asparagus	
1 tsp. salt	
1 tsp. sugar	
1 onion	
2 tbs. butter	
3 tbs. flour	
½ cup hot veal stock	
½ cup hot milk	
⅛ tsp. salt	
⅛ tsp. nutmeg	
⅛ tsp. white pepper	
⅛ tsp. dried thyme	
½ cup grated Gruyère cheese	
2 egg yolks	
¼ cup whipping cream	

Prepare and cook asparagus following directions in Classic Asparagus. Drain well. • Peel and finely dice onion. • Melt butter in a large saucepan. Add diced onion and sauté until transparent. Add flour and sauté until golden. Slowly pour in veal stock and bring to a boil. Stir in hot milk and bring sauce to a boil again. Remove from heat and season with salt, nutmeg, pepper and thyme. Add grated cheese. • Whisk egg yolks and cream together. Gradually stir ¼ cup of hot sauce into egg and cream mixture. Stir egg yolk into sauce. • Preheat oven to 450°F. • Place cooked asparagus in an oven-proof dish and cover with cheese sauce. Bake for 10 to 15 minutes.

Classic Asparagus
(upper right photograph)

470 calories per serving
Preparation time: 15 minutes
Cooking time: 15 to 20 minutes

3⅓ lbs. white asparagus	
1 tsp. salt	
1 tsp. sugar	
7 tbs. butter	

Thinly peel each asparagus spear from top to bottom with a vegetable peeler. Cut off bottom part of stalk. Rinse asparagus spears with cold water. Tie in bundles of 6 to 10 spears. • Fill a large saucepan with enough water to cover asparagus bundles. Add salt and sugar and bring to a boil. Place asparagus bundles in boiling water and cook, covered, for 15 to 20 minutes, until asparagus spears are just tender. • Melt butter, transfer to a sauce dish and keep warm over very low heat. • Remove cooked asparagus from water and briefly dip in freshly boiled salt water. Drain asparagus bundles on a thick layer of paper towels. • To serve, separate asparagus and arrange on a warmed serving platter. Garnish as desired.

Hash Brown Potatoes

490 calories per serving
Preparation time: 20 minutes
Cooking time: 40 to 45 minutes

1¾ lbs. potatoes
4 strips bacon
2 large onions
½ cup flour
2 eggs
1 tsp. salt
⅛ tsp. white pepper
½ tsp. dried, or 2 tbs. fresh, marjoram
⅓ cup bread crumbs
3 tbs. vegetable oil

Place potatoes in a large saucepan with water to cover. Boil, covered, cook for 30 to 35 minutes, or until tender. Drain and cool. • Dice bacon. Peel and finely chop onion. Peel and grate potatoes. • Sauté bacon in a frying pan until crisp. Add chopped onion and sauté until transparent. Combine with potatoes. Stir in flour, eggs, salt, pepper and marjoram to form a batter. • Shape batter into 1– × 2-inch patties and coat with bread crumbs. • Heat vegetable oil in a large frying pan. Add potato patties and fry on all sides until brown and crispy. Drain on paper towels. Serve at once.

Potato Pancakes on Spinach

365 calories per serving
Preparation time: 30 minutes
Cooking time: 20 minutes

¾ to 1 lb. potatoes
3 tbs. flour
1¾ tsp. salt
1 lb. spinach
⅛ tsp. nutmeg
4 tbs. clarified butter
4 strips bacon
4 eggs
⅛ tsp. coarsely ground black pepper

Peel, wash and grate potatoes. Combine grated potatoes with flour and 1 teaspoon of salt. Cover and set aside. • Preheat oven to 250°F. Sort and wash spinach. Place wet spinach in a large ovenproof pan and steam, covered, over low heat for 10 minutes, or until wilted. Season with ½ teaspoon of salt and nutmeg. Cover and keep warm in oven. • Divide potato mixture into 4 portions. Melt 1 tablespoon of clarified butter in a frying pan. Add 1 portion of potatoes and fry until crispy and brown on both sides. Keep warm in oven while frying remaining 3 potato pancakes. • Sauté bacon in same frying pan until crisp. Remove bacon and keep warm in oven. • Fry 4 eggs, sunny-side-up, in bacon fat. Sprinkle each egg with salt and coarsely ground black pepper. • To serve, divide spinach among 4 plates. Cover with a potato pancake, then a fried egg and a strip of bacon.

Potatoes and Peas in Béchamel Sauce

405 calories per serving
Preparation time: 15 minutes
Cooking time: 30 to 35 minutes

2¼ lbs. potatoes
1⅓ lbs. fresh peas
½ cup water
⅛ tsp. salt
1 cup mixed herbs, such as dill, chervil, lovage, parsley and chives
1 onion
2 tbs. butter
1 tbs. flour
½ cup hot milk
⅛ tsp. salt
⅛ tsp. white pepper
¼ cup whipping cream

Place potatoes in a saucepan and cover with water. Boil gently for 30 to 35 minutes. Drain, peel and slice potatoes. • Shell peas and boil in salted water for 6 to 9 minutes. Drain, reserving liquid. Place cooked peas in a bowl, cover and set aside. • Wash, dry and chop herbs. Peel and dice onion. • Melt butter in a large saucepan. Add onion and sauté until transparent. Add flour and sauté, stirring constantly, until light yellow. Stir in reserved cooking liquid and hot milk. Simmer sauce for three minutes. Season with salt and white pepper. • Add potatoes and peas to sauce and cook until heated through. • To serve, stir in cream and sprinkle with herbs.

Tip: The peas may be replaced by green beans or diced green pepper. Add sautéed, diced bacon or smoked sausage slices for a heartier dish.

Stuffed Green Peppers
(lower right photograph)

515 calories per serving
Preparation time: 20 minutes
Cooking time: 40 minutes

4 large green peppers
1½ tsp. salt
1 large onion
2 cloves garlic
¼ lb. mushrooms
2 tbs. vegetable oil
½ lb. ground beef
½ lb. ground pork
1 cup cooked long-grain rice
1 egg
½ tsp. dried rosemary
2 tbs. chopped parsley
1 cup hot meat stock
¼ cup tomato paste
7 tbs. sour cream
⅛ tsp. sugar
⅛ tsp. paprika

Cut a thin slice off top of each pepper. Remove membrane and seeds. Wash pepper cases and sprinkle insides with salt. • Peel and finely chop onion and garlic cloves. Clean and thinly slice mushrooms. • Heat vegetable oil in large frying pan. Add onion and garlic and sauté until transparent. Add mushrooms and ground meats. Sauté briefly, stirring constantly. Add rice, remaining salt, egg, rosemary and parsley. • Fill pepper cases with meat and rice mixture. Place in a large saucepan, pour in hot meat stock and steam, covered, over low heat for 40 minutes. • Transfer stuffed peppers to a serving platter and keep warm. Stir tomato paste and sour cream into pan with meat stock. Season with sugar and paprika. Serve sauce with stuffed peppers.

Peppers Stuffed with Crushed Grains
(upper left photograph)

310 calories per serving
Preparation time: 20 minutes
Cooking time: 40 minutes

4 large red peppers
1 large onion
4 small tomatoes
1 tbs. vegetable oil
½ cup freshly crushed, 6-grain mixture
2 eggs
¼ cup chopped mixed herbs
1 tsp. salt
⅛ tsp. cayenne
1 cup hot vegetable stock
2 tbs. sour cream
¼ cup grated Swiss cheese
2 tbs. chopped sunflower seeds
1 tsp. cornstarch
¼ cup orange juice

Cut a thin slice off top of each pepper to use as a lid. Remove membrane and seeds. Peel and finely dice onion. Peel and dice tomatoes. • Heat vegetable oil in a frying pan. Add onion and sauté until transparent. Add crushed grain and sauté briefly. Remove pan from heat and add tomatoes, eggs, herbs and spices. • Fill the pepper cases with grain mixture. Place in a large saucepan and pour in vegetable stock. Combine sour cream, cheese and sunflower seeds and spread over stuffing. Replace pepper lids. Steam peppers, covered, over low heat for 40 minutes. Remove from pan and keep warm. • Dissolve cornstarch in orange juice. Add to cooking liquid, stirring constantly. Boil briefly, until sauce thickens. Season with salt and cayenne. Serve immediately, with stuffed peppers.

Stuffed Cucumbers

475 calories per serving
Preparation time: 30 minutes
Cooking time: 30 minutes

4 cucumbers
¼ cup flour
⅓ cup vegetable oil
3 hard-boiled eggs
¼ cup whipping cream
⅛ tsp. white pepper
⅛ tsp. salt
⅛ tsp. nutmeg
1 tbs. chopped dill
1 tbs. chopped parsley
⅔ lb. lean, cooked ham
2 onions
½ cup hot poultry stock
Fresh dill

Peel, wash and dry cucumbers. Cut off upper third to use as a lid and scrape out seeds with a spoon. Roll cucumbers in flour. • Heat 2 tablespoons vegetable oil in a Dutch oven. Add cucumbers and sauté on all sides. Remove from the pot. • Peel eggs. Combine egg yolks, cream, spices and herbs. Set aside. • Finely dice ham. Peel and finely dice onions. Heat 1 tablespoon of vegetable oil in frying pan. Add onions and sauté until golden. Add diced ham and continue to sauté, stirring frequently. Cool, then add to egg mixture. • Finely chop egg whites and add to filling. Fill cucumbers with filling and place lids on top. • Heat remaining vegetable oil in Dutch oven. Lay cucumbers in oil. Pour stock around cucumbers and simmer, covered, over low heat for 30 minutes. • To serve, garnish cucumbers with dill.

Stuffed Kohlrabi

350 calories per serving
Preparation time: 20 minutes
Cooking time: 40 minutes

4 large kohlrabies
2 cups vegetable stock
2 shallots
½ cup wheatgerm
¼ cup chopped cashews
2 eggs
1 tsp. salt
1 tbs. chopped parsley
7 tbs. sour cream
1 tsp. cornstarch

Wash and peel kohlrabies. Chop tender leaves and set aside. • Place whole kohlrabies and vegetable stock in a large saucepan and cook, covered, for 25 minutes. Drain, reserving stock, and cool. • Slice off top third of kohlrabies and hollow out bottom third. Chop kohlrabi pulp and cut-off top pieces. Peel and chop shallots and combine with the chopped kohlrabi, wheatgerm, cashews, eggs, salt and parsley. Spoon filling into kohlrabi cases. • Place stuffed kohlrabies in a large saucepan and pour in half the vegetable stock. Cook, covered, for 15 minutes. • Transfer kohlrabies to a warm serving dish. • Strain cooking liquid and mix with sour cream. Dissolve cornstarch in a little cold water. Add cornstarch to sauce, stirring constantly. Bring to a boil. Season with salt to taste and add chopped kohlrabi leaves. To serve, pour sauce over stuffed kohlrabies.

Mushroom Stuffed Potatoes

345 calories per serving
Preparation time: 35 minutes
Cooking time: 35 minutes

½ lb. mushrooms	
1 large onion	
2 tbs. vegetable oil	
1 tbs. chopped parsley	
⅛ tsp. salt	
⅛ tsp. white pepper	
1 small egg	
2 tbs. bread crumbs	
8 large, equal-sized potatoes	
2 cups vegetable stock	
1 tbs. flour	
½ cup sour cream	
⅛ tsp. salt	
⅛ tsp. white pepper	

Clean and finely chop mushrooms. Peel and dice onions. Heat 1 tablespoon of vegetable oil in a saucepan. Add onions and sauté until transparent. Add mushrooms and parsley and steam, covered, over low heat for 5 minutes. Remove vegetables from heat and season with salt and pepper. Cool slightly. Mix in egg and just enough bread crumbs to make a workable stuffing. • Peel potatoes. Cut off top third of each potato to use as a lid. Hollow out insides of bottom parts and fill with mushroom stuffing. Place lids on top and tie with string. Heat remaining vegetable oil in saucepan and sauté potatoes on all sides. Heat vegetable stock in a separate pan and pour over potatoes. Simmer, covered, for 35 minutes. • Remove potatoes from cooking liquid and keep warm. Combine the flour with a little cold water and stir until dissolved. Add flour mixture to cooking liquid, stirring constantly until sauce thickens. Stir in sour cream and season with salt and pepper. • Remove strings from potatoes to serve. Serve with sauce on the side.

Stuffed Eggplant

400 calories per serving
Preparation time: 30 minutes
Cooking time: 40 minutes

2 medium-sized eggplants	
½ tsp. salt	
4 strips bacon	
2 onions	
1 clove garlic	
4 tomatoes	
½ lb. mushrooms	
1½ cups cooked long-grain rice	
½ tsp. salt	
½ tsp. paprika	
⅛ tsp. pepper	
⅛ tsp. ground caraway	
1 tbs. chopped parsley	
¼ cup grated Swiss cheese	
1½ cups hot stock	
7 tbs. sour cream	
2 tsp. cornstarch	
3 tbs. tomato paste	
⅛ tsp. sugar	

Cut eggplants in half lengthwise, scrape out pulp and chop finely. Salt insides of eggplant cases. Dice bacon. Peel and finely chop onions and garlic cloves. Peel and dice tomatoes. Clean mushrooms and slice thinly. • Preheat oven to 400°F. • Place bacon in a saucepan and sauté until crisp. Add onions, garlic, mushrooms and eggplant pulp and stir-fry briefly. Add tomatoes and steam, covered, over low heat for 5 minutes. Mix in rice and season with spices and parsley. •

Place eggplant cases in an oven-proof dish. Spoon filling into cases. Sprinkle with cheese and pour in vegetable stock. Bake for 40 minutes. Remove from pan and keep warm. • Whisk cooking liquid, sour cream, tomato paste and sugar together. Boil briefly and serve with stuffed eggplants.

Creamed Potatoes and Carrots
(left photograph)

350 calories per serving
Preparation time: 20 minutes
Cooking time: 25 minutes

1¾ lbs. carrots
3 green onions
1 lb. potatoes
3 tbs. margarine
2 tbs. maple syrup
1 cup hot vegetable stock
1 tsp. salt
½ cup whipping cream
2 tbs. chopped chives

Scrape carrots and cut into uniform cubes. Wash, trim and slice onions. Peel, wash and dice potatoes. • Melt margarine in a large saucepan. Stir in maple syrup. Add sliced onion and carrots and sauté for 5 minutes until caramelized, stirring frequently. Add potatoes and vegetable stock. Cover and cook, covered, over low heat for 25 minutes. Season with salt. • To serve, whip cream until stiff. Place a dollop of whipped cream on top of vegetables and sprinkle with chopped chives.

Tip: White onions can be substituted for green onions for a milder taste.

Carrots and Mangoes with Pork Tenderloin
(right photograph)

510 calories per serving
Preparation time: 30 minutes
Cooking time: 25 minutes

1⅓ lbs. pork tenderloin
2 onions
1⅔ lbs. carrots
1 large, ripe mango
⅓ cup raisins
3 tbs. freshly squeezed orange juice
2 cups meat stock
3 tbs. safflower oil
1 tbs. flour
⅛ tsp. salt
⅛ tsp. cayenne
⅛ tsp. sugar

Wash, dry and cut meat into small cubes. Peel and dice onion. Scrape and slice carrots. Cut mango in half, removing pit. Peel and dice mango halves. Soak raisins in orange juice. Heat stock in saucepan. • Heat safflower oil in large saucepan. Add onions and sauté until transparent. Add meat cubes and sauté until light brown, stirring constantly. Add carrots and flour. Gradually pour in hot stock and simmer, covered, for 20 minutes. • Season carrots with salt, cayenne and sugar. To serve, add diced mango, raisins and orange juice and simmer very gently for 5 minutes.

Leek and Tomato Omelette
(lower middle photograph)

335 calories per serving
Preparation time: 20 minutes
Cooking time: 25 minutes

3 leeks
4 large tomatoes
4 cooked potatoes (about 1 lb.)
1 large onion
3 tbs. safflower oil
½ tsp. salt
2 eggs
⅛ tsp. salt
⅛ tsp. hot paprika
¼ cup sour cream
3 tbs. chopped chives

Trim leeks, removing stem and green parts. Wash, dry and cut white parts into rings. Peel tomatoes and cut each into 8 wedges. Peel and slice potatoes. Peel and chop onion. • Heat safflower oil in a frying pan with lid. Add onion and leek and sauté until onions are transparent. Add potatoes. Sprinkle with salt and fry for 8 minutes, stirring frequently. • Add tomato wedges, cover, and steam over low heat for 15 minutes. • Whisk eggs, salt, paprika and sour cream together and fold into vegetables. Cook over moderate heat until eggs are firm. Sprinkle with chopped chives.

Fried Pumpkin Sandwiches
(upper right photograph)

515 calories per serving
Preparation and cooking time: 50 minutes

2¼ lbs. firm, peeled pumpkin
1 tsp. salt
8 cups water
1 lb. cheddar cheese
¾ cup sour cream
¼ cup chopped chives
¼ cup flour
1 egg
1 egg yolk
⅔ cup bread crumbs
6 tbs. olive oil

Cut pumpkin into uniform, ¼-inch slices. • Place salt and water in a saucepan and bring to a boil. Add pumpkin slices and blanch for 5 minutes. Remove from water and drain. • Grate cheese and combine with sour cream. • Spread cheese mixture on half of the pumpkin slices and place remaining pumpkin slices on top. Coat pumpkin sandwiches with flour. • Whisk egg, egg yolk and 1 to 2 tablespoons of sour cream together. Dip floured pumpkin sandwiches in egg mixture, then in bread crumbs. Press gently to make bread crumbs stick. Set aside to dry for several minutes. • Heat olive oil in a frying pan. Add pumpkin sandwiches, one at a time, and brown on both sides. • Keep sandwiches warm in oven until all have been fried.

Chinese Cabbage

230 calories per serving
Preparation time: 30 minutes
Cooking time: 25 minutes

| 2 dried Chinese mushrooms |
| 3⅓ lbs. Chinese cabbage |
| 2 green peppers |
| ¼ cup vegetable oil |
| ½ cup hot vegetable stock |
| ½ lb. fresh shrimp, peeled and deveined |
| 1 tbs. cornstarch |
| 1 tbs. wine vinegar |
| 2 tbs. soy sauce |
| ⅛ tsp. salt |
| ⅛ tsp. sugar |

Soak dried mushrooms in hot water for 20 minutes. Drain and cut into strips. • Cut cabbage leaves from ribs and store leaves to use another time in a salad. Wash, dry and slice ribs into 1-inch wide strips. • Cut peppers in half, remove membrane and seeds, and dice. • Heat ⅛ cup of vegetable oil in a saucepan. Add cabbage strips and sauté. Add diced peppers and sauté briefly. Pour in vegetable stock and bring to a boil. Cover and simmer for about 20 minutes, or until vegetables are transparent. • Remove vegetables from stock and keep warm. Reserve stock. • Heat remaining ⅛ cup of vegetable oil in a frying pan. Add mushrooms and shrimp and sauté until shrimp turn pink. Pour in vegetable stock and bring to a boil. Cover and simmer for 5 minutes. • Combine cornstarch, vinegar and soy sauce, stirring until cornstarch is dissolved. Add to cooking liquid, stirring constantly until liquid has thickened. Season with salt and sugar. Add vegetables and reheat.

Belgian Endive with Fish Fillets

320 calories per serving
Preparation time: 15 minutes
Cooking time: 20 minutes

| 1⅓ lbs. haddock fillets |
| 4 cups water |
| 1 tsp. salt |
| 1 tbs. lemon juice |
| ½ bay leaf |
| 2 white peppercorns |
| 1¾ lbs. Belgian endive |
| 2 onions |
| 2 tbs. safflower oil |
| ½ cup whipping cream |
| ⅛ tsp. salt |
| ⅛ tsp. white pepper |
| 2 tsp. curry |
| 1 tbs. chopped parsley |

Wash fish fillets. Place water, salt, lemon juice, bay leaf and peppercorns in a large saucepan and bring to a boil. Add fish fillets and simmer for 8 minutes. • Trim Belgian endive and cut out core. Wash, dry and slice into 1-inch wide strips. • Remove fish fillets from pan and cut into 1½-inch pieces. Reserve ½ cup of cooking liquid. • Heat safflower oil in a saucepan. Add onions and sauté until golden. Add Belgian endive and continue to sauté. Pour reserved cooking liquid over vegetables and steam, covered, over low heat for 8 minutes. • Combine whipping cream, salt, pepper and curry and stir into vegetables. Add fish pieces, cover and reheat gently, being careful not to boil. • To serve, sprinkle with parsley.

Fennel in Tomato Sauce

360 calories per serving
Preparation time: 10 minutes
Cooking time: 25 minutes

4 fennel bulbs (about 2¼ lbs.)
2 tbs. vegetable oil
1 cup poultry stock
½ cup white wine
3 tbs. tomato paste
1 tbs. flour
⅛ tsp. oregano
⅛ tsp. dried basil
½ lb. lean, cooked ham
⅛ tsp. white pepper
⅛ tsp. sugar
2 tbs. freshly grated Parmesan cheese

Remove outer leaves from fennel bulbs. Cut off tender greens, wash, dry and chop finely. Place in a covered bowl and set aside. • Trim stalks from bulbs and cut each fennel bulb in half. • Heat vegetable oil in a Dutch oven. Add fennel and brown on both sides. Heat poultry stock in a saucepan. Pour stock and wine over fennel and bring to a boil. Cover and simmer for about 25 minutes, or until tender. • Remove bulbs from liquid and keep warm. Reserve cooking liquid. • Combine tomato paste and flour and stir into cooking liquid. Cook gently for 3 minutes, stirring constantly. Add dried herbs. Dice and add ham. Season with pepper and sugar. • Arrange fennel bulbs in a serving dish. Pour ham sauce over fennel and sprinkle with Parmesan cheese. • Serve with rice garnished with reserved chopped fennel greens.

Fennel with Cooked Ham

445 calories per serving
Preparation time: 10 minutes
Cooking time: 35 minutes

2¼ lbs. fennel	
4 cups water	
⅔ lb. cooked ham	
2 tbs. butter	
1 tbs. flour	
4 tsp. sweet red wine	
¼ cup whipping cream	
⅛ tsp. salt	
⅛ tsp. white pepper	

Cut tender greens off fennel bulbs. Wash, dry and chop greens. Place in a covered bowl and set aside. • Remove outer leaves from bulbs and trim stalks. Quarter bulbs and cut into strips.

Place salt water in a large saucepan and bring to a boil. Add fennel strips and simmer for about 25 minutes, or until tender. Remove from heat and drain fennel strips, reserving 3 cups of cooking liquid. • Cut cooked ham into 1-inch strips. • Melt butter in a saucepan, add flour and sauté until golden, stirring constantly. Gradually stir in reserved cooking liquid and cook over low heat for 5 minutes, stirring vigorously. Add wine and whipping cream. Season with salt and pepper. • Add fennel and ham strips and simmer gently for 5 minutes. • To serve, garnish vegetables with reserved chopped fennel greens.

Black Salsify with Ham and Cheese

515 calories per serving
Preparation time: 10 minutes
Cooking time: 45-50 minutes

6 cups water	
¼ cup vinegar	
2 tbs. flour	
2¼ lbs. black salsify	
1 tsp. salt	
¼ cup lemon juice	
1 onion	
½ lb. lean, cooked ham	
5 tomatoes	
1 tbs. butter	
1 tsp. anchovy paste	
⅛ tsp. white pepper	
⅛ tsp. nutmeg	
⅛ tsp. Worcestershire sauce	
½ tsp. dried basil	
1 cup coarsely grated Swiss cheese	

Combine 2 cups of water, vinegar and flour in a bowl. • Brush salsify under running water. Peel, trim and rinse once more. Immediately place roots in water and flour mixture to avoid discoloration. • Combine 4 cups of water, salt and lemon juice in a large saucepan and bring to a boil. Add salsify roots and simmer for 35 to 40 minutes. • Peel and finely dice onion. Dice ham. Peel and dice tomatoes. • Preheat oven to 450°F. • Melt butter in a frying pan. Add onion and ham and sauté until onion is transparent. Add diced tomatoes, anchovy paste, spices and basil. • Drain roots, reserving liquid. Place roots in an ovenproof dish. Measure out ½ cup of cooking liquid and stir into tomato mixture. Pour tomato sauce over roots and sprinkle with cheese. • Bake on middle rack of oven for 10 minutes.

Stuffed Cabbage Leaves
(top left photograph)

565 calories per serving
Preparation time: 20 minutes
Cooking time: 1 hour

| 1 head cabbage |
| 1 tsp. salt |
| 2 onions |
| 1 clove garlic |
| 1 lb. ground lamb |
| ½ cup cooked brown rice |
| 1 egg |
| 1 tsp. lemon juice |
| ½ tsp. dried thyme |
| ⅛ tsp. white pepper |
| 2 tbs. safflower oil |
| 1 parsnip |
| 1 bay leaf |
| 1 cup hot vegetable stock |
| 1 sprig of fresh rosemary |
| 1 tbs. flour |

| 7 tbs. sour cream |
| 2 tbs. chopped parsley |

Trim cabbage. Place water to cover cabbage and salt in a large saucepan and bring to a boil. Add cabbage and boil for 10 minutes. • Peel and finely dice onions and garlic. Mix onions, garlic, lamb, rice, egg, lemon juice, thyme, salt to taste, and pepper together. Select 16 large leaves for cabbage rolls. Finely chop remaining cabbage. Place 2 leaves on top of each other, then divide filling among the 8 pairs of cabbage leaves. Fold sides of leaves over filling, roll up and tie with string. • Heat safflower oil in a Dutch oven. Add cabbage rolls and sauté until browned. • Finely chop parsnip. Add parsnip, remaining cabbage, bay leaf, stock and rosemary. Simmer, cov-

ered, over low heat for 50 minutes. • Combine flour and sour cream and add to sauce, stirring constantly until thickened. To serve, garnish with parsley.

Red Cabbage Leaves Stuffed With Chicken
(bottom right photograph)

420 calories per serving
Preparation time: 30 minutes
Cooking time: 55 minutes

| 1¾ lbs. head red cabbage |
| 1 tsp. salt |
| 1 tbs. vinegar |
| 1 lb. chicken breasts |
| 1 slice bread |
| 4 strips bacon |
| 1 onion |
| 1 carrot |
| 1 tbs. butter |
| ⅛ tsp. allspice |
| ⅛ tsp. white pepper |

| 3 tbs. vegetable oil |
| ½ cup dry red wine |
| ½ cup hot vegetable stock |
| ⅛ tsp. pepper |
| 2 tsp. red currant jelly |

Place water to cover cabbage, 1 teaspoon of salt and vinegar in a large saucepan and bring to a boil. Add red cabbage and boil for 15 minutes. • Select 16 large leaves for the cabbage rolls. Finely chop remaining cabbage. • Finely chop chicken. Soak bread in cold water. Squeeze out. Dice bacon, onion and carrot. • Melt butter in a frying pan. Add diced cabbage, bacon, onion and carrot and sauté. Add allspice, salt to taste, white pepper, bread and chopped chicken. • Divide filling among cabbage leaves. Roll up cabbage leaves and tie with string. Heat vegetable oil in a frying pan. Add cabbage rolls and cook until

browned. Transfer rolls to an ovenproof dish. • Preheat the oven to 400°F. • Pour red wine over cabbage rolls and bake for 40 minutes. • Remove the cabbage rolls from pan, pour in vegetable stock and stir until a gravy is formed. Season with ⅛ teaspoon salt, pepper and red currant jelly. • Serve cabbage rolls with gravy.

Kale with Chestnuts
(top photograph)

560 calories per serving
Preparation time: 15 minutes
Cooking time: 1 hour, 30 minutes

2¼ lbs. kale	
12 cups water	
1½ tsp. salt	
2 onions	
4 tbs. butter	
2 cups hot meat stock	

⅛ tsp. black pepper	
⅛ tsp. allspice	
1 lb. chestnuts	
1 tbs. sugar	
½ cup whipping cream	

Remove thick stalks and hard ribs from kale. Place 8 cups of water and 1 teaspoon of salt in a saucepan and bring to a boil. Add kale and boil for 5 minutes. Drain, cool slightly and chop coarsely. • Peel and dice onions. Melt 2 tablespoons of butter in a large saucepan. Add onions and sauté until transparent. Add kale, meat stock, ½ teaspoon of salt, pepper, and allspice. Simmer, covered, for 1½ hours. • Bring 4 cups of water to a boil in a separate saucepan. Score pointed ends of chestnuts with a cross and cook in rapidly boiling water for 20 to 25 minutes. Remove from pan and peel. • Melt 2 table-

spoons of butter in a frying pan. Add sugar, stirring constantly until caramelized. Turn chestnuts in caramel. Cover and keep warm over very low heat. • Combine cooked kale with whipping cream. Season to taste and fold in chestnuts.

Turnips With Lamb Chops
(bottom photograph)

675 calories per serving
Preparation time: 15 minutes
Cooking time: 45 minutes

3⅓ lbs. turnips	
3 onions	
2 tbs. vegetable shortening	
1 tbs. sugar	
2 cups hot meat stock	
1 tsp. salt	
½ tsp. white pepper	

1 tsp. dried marjoram	
1 tbs. chopped parsley	
4 lamb loin chops (3½ oz. each)	
2 tbs. vegetable oil	

Scrub turnips, peel, and trim off woody parts. Dice turnips. Peel and dice onions. • Heat shortening in a large saucepan. Add onions and sauté until transparent. Add turnips, sprinkle with sugar and turn in hot shortening until sugar has caramelized. Pour in the stock and season with salt, pepper and marjoram. Simmer, covered, for 45 minutes. • Score edges of lamb chops so chops do not curl up when fried. Heat vegetable oil in a frying pan. Add lamb chops and fry 4 minutes on each side. Season each chop with salt and white pepper to taste. • Sprinkle turnips with parsley and serve with lamb chops.

Green Bean and Beef Stew

460 calories per serving
Preparation time: 30 minutes
Cooking time: 45 minutes

1 lb. green beans
1 lb. potatoes
2 onions
1⅓ lbs. stew beef
2 tbs. vegetable oil
1 cup hot meat stock
½ tsp. salt
⅛ tsp. white pepper
3 tbs. tomato paste
2 sprigs of summer savory
1 lb. tomatoes
½ tsp. dried rosemary
2 tbs. chopped parsley

String beans, rinse with cold water and cut into 1½-inch pieces. Peel, wash and dice potatoes. Peel and dice onions. Cut beef into uniform cubes. • Heat vegetable oil in a large saucepan. Add onions and sauté until transparent. Add meat and brown on all sides for 7 to 8 minutes, turning constantly. Pour in meat stock. Add salt, pepper and tomato paste. Add summer savory and simmer, covered, for 15 minutes. • Add beans and diced potatoes and cook 20 minutes longer. • Peel tomatoes and cut into eighths. Add tomato pieces and rosemary to vegetables and simmer 10 minutes. • Remove summer savory and garnish stew with parsley.

Cucumbers with Poultry Dumplings

465 calories per serving
Preparation time: 20 minutes
Cooking time: 30 minutes

2¼ lbs. cucumbers
1 lb. potatoes
2 onions
2 cloves garlic
1⅓ lbs. poultry breasts
⅛ tsp. salt
⅛ tsp. paprika
1 egg
⅓ cup bread crumbs
2 tbs. safflower oil
2 cups hot vegetable stock
½ tsp. salt
⅛ tsp. black pepper
2 tbs. tomato ketchup
¼ cup sour cream
2 tbs. chopped parsley

Peel cucumbers and cut in half lengthwise. Scrape out seeds and slice cucumber halves. Peel, wash and dice potatoes. Peel and finely chop onions and garlic. • Grind poultry breasts, season with salt and paprika, and knead together with egg and bread crumbs. Cover and set aside. • Heat safflower oil in a saucepan. Add onions and garlic and sauté until onions are transparent. Add cucumber slices and stir-fry. Add diced potatoes and vegetable stock and bring to a boil. Cover and simmer for 30 minutes. • Shape ground poultry mixture into walnut-sized balls and simmer in very gently boiling salt water for 10 minutes. • Season vegetables with salt and pepper. Stir in ketchup and sour cream. • To serve, arrange poultry dumplings on vegetables and sprinkle with parsley.

Young Turnips with Chicken Legs
(right photograph)

430 calories per serving
Preparation time: 10 minutes
Cooking time: 40 minutes

2¼ lbs. young turnips	
1 bunch of soup greens	
3 cups vegetable stock	
4 chicken legs (6½ oz. each)	
1⅓ lbs. potatoes	
½ tsp. salt	
⅛ tsp. white pepper	
⅛ tsp. cayenne	
4 shallots	
2 tbs. vegetable oil	
2 tbs. chopped parsley	

Peel and cut turnips into cubes. Trim, wash and coarsely chop soup greens. Combine turnips, soup greens and vegetable stock in a large saucepan and bring to a boil. Cover and simmer for 40 minutes. • Wash and dry chicken legs. Peel, wash and dice the potatoes. Add chicken legs, diced potatoes, salt, pepper and cayenne to turnips after 20 minutes of cooking time. Cook, covered, 20 minutes longer. • Peel shallots and slice into rings. • Heat vegetable oil in a frying pan. Add shallots and sauté until golden brown. • To serve, garnish with sautéed shallots and parsley.

Kohlrabi With Cheese Sauce
(left photograph)

450 calories per serving
Preparation time: 20 minutes
Cooking time: 30 minutes

4 large kohlrabies	
2 onions	
1 lb. new potatoes	
2 tbs. vegetable oil	
1 cup vegetable stock	
1 tbs. flour	
½ tsp. salt	
⅛ tsp. white pepper	
⅛ tsp. sugar	
2 egg yolks	
½ cup whipping cream	
1 cup freshly grated Gouda cheese	
2 tbs. chopped lovage	

Peel, wash and cut kohlrabi into julienne pieces, reserving tender kohlrabi leaves. Chop leaves, cover and set aside. • Peel and dice onions. Wash potatoes and drop in boiling water to cover. Cook, covered, for 30 minutes, or until tender. • Heat vegetable oil in a saucepan. Add diced onions and sauté until transparent. Add julienned kohlrabi, sauté briefly, then pour in ½ cup of vegetable stock. Simmer, covered, over low heat for 15 minutes. • Combine flour with remaining cold vegetable stock, stirring until flour dissolves. Add to cooking liquid, stirring constantly until sauce has thickened. Cook vegetables a 3 minutes more, stirring occasionally. • Drain potatoes, peel and slice. Combine with kohlrabi. Season with salt, pepper and sugar. • Mix egg yolks, whipping cream and grated cheese together and stir into kohlrabi. Sprinkle with chopped lovage and kohlrabi leaves.

Stuffed Spinach Leaves

280 calories per serving
Preparation time: 45 minutes
Cooking time: 15 minutes

1 lb. mushrooms
2 tbs. butter
¼ tsp. salt
⅛ teaspoon Tabasco sauce
½ cup vegetable stock
1 cup soft, crustless white bread crumbs
1 egg
1⅓ lbs. large spinach leaves
1 onion
⅛ tsp. nutmeg
7 tbs. sour cream
2 tbs. freshly grated Parmesan cheese

Clean and chop mushrooms. Melt 1 tablespoon of butter in a saucepan. Add mushrooms and sauté, stirring constantly. Season with ⅛ teaspoon salt and Tabasco sauce. Add 6 tablespoons of vegetable stock and steam mushrooms, uncovered, over low heat for 5 minutes. • Soak bread crumbs in remaining vegetable stock. Add bread crumbs to mushrooms, then mix in egg. Set stuffing aside. • Remove large spinach stalks and wash leaves. Blanch spinach in boiling salt water for 5 minutes. Drain. Combine spinach leaves to make 8 squares measuring 4 x 6 inches. Coarsely chop remaining spinach. • Peel and finely dice onion. Melt 1 tablespoon of butter in a saucepan. Add onion and sauté until transparent. Add chopped spinach, season with ⅛ teaspoon salt and nutmeg and steam briefly. Transfer spinach to an ovenproof dish. • Preheat oven to 400°F. • Divide mushroom stuffing among spinach leaves. Roll leaves up, folding in the sides. Arrange spinach rolls in ovenproof dish. Place sour cream and Parmesan cheese on top. Bake for 15 minutes.

Asparagus Casserole

370 calories per serving
Preparation time: 30 minutes
Cooking time: 30 minutes

2¼ lbs. asparagus	
8 cups water	
1½ tsp. salt	
1 tsp. sugar	
½ lb. lean, cooked ham	
1 tbs. butter	
1 tbs. flour	
½ cup milk	
⅛ tsp. white pepper	
⅛ tsp. paprika	
1 cup freshly grated Swiss cheese	
2 egg yolks	

Wash asparagus and cut off woody part of stalks. Tie into 4 bundles. Combine water, 1 teaspoon of salt and sugar in a large saucepan and bring to a boil. Add asparagus bundles and simmer, covered, for 10 minutes. • Cut ham into 1-inch strips. • Pre heat oven to 400°F. Grease a casserole dish with butter. • Drain asparagus, reserving cooking liquid, and remove string. Arrange asparagus in casserole dish and sprinkle ham strips on top. • Melt butter in a saucepan. Add flour and sauté until golden, stirring constantly. Pour in ½ cup of asparagus cooking liquid and milk. Season with ½ teaspoon of salt, pepper and paprika. Cook over low heat for 5 minutes, stirring constantly. Remove from heat and cool slightly. Stir in cheese and egg yolks and pour sauce over asparagus. Place casserole in oven and bake for 20 minutes.

Zucchini Casserole

375 calories per serving
Preparation time: 30 minutes
Cooking time: 20 minutes

1 onion	
2 cloves garlic	
1⅓ lbs. tomatoes	
1¾ ozs. dandelion leaves	
3 tbs. safflower oil	
1 tsp. salt	
1 tsp. chopped rosemary	
1 tsp. honey	
⅛ tsp. cayenne	
2¼ lbs. small zucchini	
7 tbs. sour cream	
1 cup wheat germ	

Peel and finely chop onion and garlic. Peel and dice tomatoes. Wash, dry and cut dandelion leaves into julienne strips. • Heat 1 tablespoon safflower oil in a saucepan. Add onion and sauté until transparent. Add tomatoes. Season with salt, rosemary, honey and cayenne. Cook, uncovered, over low heat for 10 minutes. Add dandelion leaves. • Wash and dry zucchini; cut off stems and cut into 1-inch pieces. Heat remaining safflower oil in a frying pan. Add zucchini and sauté on all sides until golden. • Preheat oven to 400°F. • Combine sour cream and wheatgerm. Place diced zucchini in oven proof dish, alternating with layers of tomato mixture. Spread sour cream mixture on top of vegetables. • Place casserole in oven and bake for 20 minutes.

Tomato and Egg Casserole

495 calories per serving
Preparation time: 15 minutes
Cooking time: 30 minutes

2 slices whole-wheat bread
2 tbs. butter
1 lb. mushrooms
2 onions
1 large clove garlic
1 tsp. salt
⅛ tsp. black pepper
2 tbs. chopped parsley
4 hard-boiled eggs
4 large tomatoes
½ cup sour cream
3 tbs. freshly grated Swiss cheese

Cut bread into uniform cubes. Melt 1 tablespoon of butter in a frying pan. Add bread cubes and sauté until crispy. Transfer croutons to a greased ovenproof dish. • Clean and thinly slice mushrooms. Peel, finely dice and sauté onions and garlic in remaining butter until transparent. Add mushrooms, salt and pepper and stir-fry for 8 minutes. • Mix in 1 tablespoon of parsley and spread mixture over croutons. • Preheat oven to 400°F. • Peel and slice eggs and place on top of mushrooms. Wash, dry and slice tomatoes and arrange in a ring around egg slices. Combine sour cream and grated cheese and pour over egg slices. • Place casserole in oven and bake for 20 minutes. • To serve, sprinkle tomato slices with remaining parsley.

Potato and Ham Casserole

580 calories per serving
Preparation time: 10 minutes
Cooking time: 55 minutes

1¾ lbs. potatoes
⅔ lb. lean, cooked ham
2 tbs. butter
1 tbs. flour
2 cups warm milk
½ tsp. salt
⅛ tsp. white pepper
⅛ tsp. nutmeg
2 egg yolks
3 tbs. germ wheat
½ cup freshly grated Swiss cheese
1 large onion
Parsley for garnish
Tomato wedges for garnish

Wash potatoes and cook, covered in boiling salted water for 30 minutes. Cool, peel and dice. • Dice ham and combine with diced potatoes. • Melt 1 tablespoon of butter in a saucepan. Add flour and sauté until golden, stirring constantly. Gradually pour in milk and cook over low heat, stirring constantly, for three minutes. • Season with salt, pepper and nutmeg. Remove from heat and stir in egg yolks. • Add potatoes and ham to sauce and pour into an ovenproof dish. • Preheat oven to 450°F. • Mix germ wheat and grated cheese together and sprinkle over potato mixture. • Place casserole on bottom rack of oven and bake for 25 minutes. • Peel and slice onion into rings. Heat 1 tablespoon of butter in a frying pan. Add onion and sauté until golden brown. • To serve, garnish with onion rings, parsley and tomato wedges.

Vegetables in a Roman Pot

545 calories per serving
Preparation time: 20 minutes
Cooking time: 1 hour

1 head cauliflower (about 2¼ lbs.)
1 lb. tomatoes
½ slice of bread
1 small onion
½ lb. ground beef
½ lb. ground pork
1 egg
⅛ tsp. white pepper
1 tsp. salt
½ cup freshly grated Parmesan cheese
2 tbs. butter
2 tbs. chopped parsley

Soak a clay pot in cold water to cover for 20 minutes. •
Wash cauliflower, trim and divide into florets. Peel and quarter tomatoes. Soak bread in cold water. Peel and finely chop onion.
• Place ground meats in a bowl. Add chopped onion, egg, pepper and ½ teaspoon of salt. Squeeze out bread and add to meat. Mix ingredients well. • Place cauliflower florets in soaked clay pot and cover with meat mixture. Place tomato quarters on top and season with salt. Sprinkle tomatoes with grated Parmesan cheese and dot with butter. • Cover clay pot and place it on a rack on bottom of a cold oven. Set oven temperature to 450°F and bake for 1 hour. • To serve, garnish with parsley.

Corn Casserole
(top photograph)

705 calories per serving
Serves: 6
Preparation time: 30 minutes
Cooking time: 40 minutes

½ cup raisins
3 large onions
2 tbs. safflower oil
¾ lb. ground beef
¾ lb. ground pork
½ to 1 cup meat stock
1 tsp. salt
¼ tsp. Tabasco sauce
2¼ lbs. canned corn
⅛ tsp. sugar
3 tbs. butter
1 tbs. chopped parsley

Soak raisins in lukewarm water. Peel and finely dice onions. • Heat safflower oil in a large frying pan. Add onions and sauté until golden, stirring frequently. Add ground meats and sauté, continually breaking meat apart. Pour in a little meat stock and season with salt and Tabasco sauce. Drain raisins and mix into meat. • Spoon meat into an ovenproof dish. Preheat oven to 400°F. • Puree corn in blender or food processor. Season with salt to taste and sugar. Pour pureed corn on top of meat and dot with butter. • Bake casserole for about 40 minutes. • To serve, sprinkle with chop parsley.

Tip: Raisins may be omited, in which case season more generously with salt and Tabasco sauce.

Leek au Gratin
(bottom photograph)

505 calories per serving
Preparation time; 20 minutes
ooking time: 1 hour

1 lb. leftover pot roast
2¼ lbs. leeks
2 tsp. salt
1 lb. potatoes
6 tbs. butter
2 egg yolks
⅛ tsp. white pepper
⅛ tsp. nutmeg
½ cup hot milk
2 tbs. chopped parsley
⅓ cup sour cream
⅓ cup bread crumbs
Butter for greasing

Cut meat into small cubes. • Trim root ends and dark leaves from leeks. Cut leeks in half lengthwise, wash thoroughly and cut into 1-inch long pieces. Place water to cover and 1 teaspoon of salt in a saucepan and bring to a boil. Add leeks and blanch for 10 minutes; drain. • Peel, wash and dice potatoes. Place in a saucepan with water to cover and 1 teaspoon of salt. Boil for 25 to 30 minutes, or until tender. • Drain potatoes, steam off moisture, and mash them. Add 2 tablespoons of butter, egg yolks, salt, pepper, nutmeg and milk. Beat vigorously with a wire whisk. • Preheat oven to 400°F. • Grease an ovenproof dish with butter. Place mashed potatoes in dish and dot with 2 tablespoons of butter. • Arrange meat, leeks and parsley on mashed potatoes. Pour sour cream on top and bake for 5 minutes. • Melt remaining butter in a frying pan. Add bread crumbs and sauté until golden brown. To serve, sprinkle with bread crumbs.

Leeks and Rice

420 calories per serving
Preparation time: 30 minutes
Cooking time: 20 to 25 minutes

2¼ lbs. leeks	
1 lb. tomatoes	
1 large onion	
4 strips bacon	
2 tbs. butter	
1 cup rice	
2 cups meat stock	
½ tsp. salt	
⅛ tsp. black pepper	
⅛ tsp. dried thyme	
2 tbs. chopped parsley	
Grated Parmesan cheese	

Trim root ends and dark green leaves from leeks. Cut leeks in half lengthwise, wash thoroughly and slice. Peel and quarter tomatoes, then halve the quarters. Peel and finely dice onion. Dice bacon. • Melt butter in a large saucepan. Add onion and sauté until transparent, stirring constantly. Add rice and sauté until transparent. Add sliced leek and sauté briefly. • Heat meat stock in a separate saucepan, then add to leek mixture. Cook over low heat for 20 to 25 minutes, adding additional water if necessary. • Mix in tomatoes 10 minutes before end of cooking period. Season with salt, pepper and thyme and continue cooking until ingredients are tender. • Sauté diced bacon in a small, dry frying pan until brown and crispy. Combine sautéed bacon and chopped parsley. To serve, mix bacon-parsley mixture into rice. Sprinkle with grated Parmesan cheese.

Eggplant and Rice Casserole

605 calories per serving
Preparation time: 30 minutes
Cooking time: 30 minutes

1 cup long-grain rice	
8 cups water	
2 tsp. salt	
1 lb. eggplant	
2 onions	
1 clove garlic	
3 tbs. safflower oil	
½ lb. ground beef	
½ lb. ground pork	
⅛ tsp. black pepper	
⅛ tsp. paprika	
½ tsp. dried basil	
4 tomatoes, sliced	
½ cup vegetable stock	
2 tbs. chopped parsley	

Combine rice, water and 1 teaspoon of salt in a saucepan. Bring to a boil, cover, and simmer for 15 minutes. • Wash, dry and trim stems off eggplant. Cut eggplant into round slices, sprinkle with 1 teaspoon of salt and set aside for 15 minutes. • Peel and finely dice onions and garlic. • Heat 1 tablespoon safflower oil in a large frying pan. Add diced onion and garlic and sauté until transparent. Add ground meat and brown thoroughly, turning constantly. Season with salt to taste, pepper, paprika and basil. • Heat remaining safflower oil in a saucepan. Blot eggplant slices, add to hot oil and fry on both sides. • Preheat oven to 400°F. • Drain rice. Spoon a layer of rice into an ovenproof dish. • Place half the eggplant on top of the rice, cover with ground meat, remaining eggplant and remaining rice. Arrange tomatoes on top of rice. Pour vegetable stock over casserole. • Bake for 30 minutes. • To serve, sprinkle with parsley.

Savoy Cabbage and Potatoes

440 calories per serving
Preparation time: 20 minutes
Cooking time: 30 minutes

2¼ lbs. savoy cabbage	
1⅓ lbs. potatoes	
1 large, tart apple	
1 tsp. lemon juice	
1 large onion	
4 tbs. safflower oil	
2 cups hot vegetable stock	
½ tsp. salt	
1 tsp. maple syrup	
1 cup sour cream	
¼ cup wheatgerm	

Trim and quarter cabbage. Remove core and cut quarters into strips. Peel and dice potatoes. Peel, core and dice apple; sprinkle with lemon juice. Peel and dice onion. • Heat 2 tablespoons safflower oil in a large saucepan. Add onion and sauté until transparent. Add cabbage strips, diced apple and potatoes, and vegetable stock. Simmer, covered, for 30 minutes. Season with salt and maple syrup. Stir in sour cream. • Heat remaining 2 tablespoons safflower oil in a frying pan. Add wheatgerm and stir-fry until golden brown. • To serve, transfer vegetables to a serving dish and sprinkle with wheat germ.

Tip: Fresh pineapple chunks can be substituted for diced apple.

Brussels Sprouts Casserole

520 calories per serving
Preparation time: 10 minutes
Cooking time: 35 minutes

| 1¾ lbs. Brussels sprouts |
| 8 cups water |
| 2 tsp. salt |
| ¾ lb. lean, cooked ham |
| ½ cup hot meat stock |
| 3 eggs |
| ½ cup milk |
| ⅛ tsp. white pepper |
| ⅛ tsp. nutmeg |
| 1 cup freshly grated Gouda cheese |

Trim and wash Brussels sprouts. Combine water and 1 teaspoon of salt in a saucepan and bring to a boil. Add Brussels sprouts and simmer, covered, for 10 minutes. Drain. • Cut ham into 1-inch strips. • Preheat oven to 450°F. • Put Brussels sprouts and half of the ham in a casserole dish. Cover with hot meat stock. • Whisk eggs, milk, 1 teaspoon of salt, pepper and nutmeg together and pour over Brussels sprouts. Arrange remaining ham strips in the middle of the Brussels sprouts and sprinkle with grated cheese. • Cover dish with aluminum foil and bake for 15 minutes. • Remove foil and bake 10 minutes longer. • Serve with fresh French bread or pan-fried potatoes.

Green Pepper Casserole

485 calories per serving
Preparation time: 20 minutes
Cooking time: 1 hour, 10 minutes

| 1¾ lbs. potatoes |
| 4 cups water |
| 1 tsp. salt |
| ⅓ lb. Italian sausage |
| 2 cloves garlic |
| 2 tbs. safflower oil |
| 2 tbs. chopped parsley |
| 4 green peppers |
| 2 eggs |
| ½ cup milk |
| ⅛ tsp. white pepper |
| 1 cup mixed herbs, such as oregano, sage and thyme |
| ½ cup freshly grated Parmesan cheese |

Wash potatoes well. Bring water and ½ teaspoon of salt to a boil in a saucepan. Add potatoes, cover, and cook over low heat for 35 minutes. Drain and cool. • Dice sausage. Peel and finely chop garlic cloves. • Heat 1 tablespoon safflower oil in a frying pan. Add sausage and garlic and sauté until sausage is brown and crispy. Mix in parsley. Remove from heat and set aside. • Quarter peppers, removing inner membrane and seeds. Cut peppers into (julienne) strips. Peel and slice potatoes. • Preheat oven to 450°F. • Whisk eggs, milk, ½ teaspoon of salt and pepper together. • Place ingredients in an ovenproof dish, alternating layers of sliced potatoes, julienned green pepper and sausage mixture. Pour in egg and milk mixture. • Cover dish with aluminum foil and bake for 30 minutes. • Wash, dry and finely chop herbs. • Sprinkle casserole with chopped herbs, Parmesan and 1 tablespoon safflower oil after 30 minutes of baking time. Bake, uncovered, for 5 minutes longer.

Black Salsify and Chicken Stew
(left photograph)

645 calories per serving
Preparation time: 30 minutes
Cooking time: 1 hour, 30 minutes

| 1 chicken, about 2¼ lbs. |
| 1 bunch of soup greens |
| 8 cups water |
| 1½ tsp. salt |
| 1 onion |
| 1 bay leaf |
| 2 cloves |
| 1¾ lbs. black salsify |
| 6 tbs. vinegar |
| 4 potatoes |
| 2 tbs. flour |
| ¼ cup milk |
| 2 tbs. small capers |
| ½ cup sour cream |
| ⅛ tsp. white pepper |

| ⅛ teaspoon Worcestershire sauce |
| ¼ cup chopped chives |

Wash chicken. Wash, trim and coarsely chop soup greens. • Combine water and 1 teaspoon of salt in a saucepan and bring to a boil. Add chicken, chicken giblets and soup greens. Skim scum that rises to surface during first 15 minutes of cooking. • Peel onion and stick it with bay leaf and cloves. Add prepared onion to chicken and simmer for 30 minutes. • Brush salsify under running water, peel and rinse again. Place roots in vinegar as they are peeled. Cut salsify into pieces 2 inches long. Add to chicken and simmer for 30 minutes. • Peel, wash and dice potatoes. Add to the chicken and simmer for 20 minutes, or until tender. • Remove chicken from stock. Remove skin and bones, then dice meat. • Strain 1 cup of stock, reserving the remaining stock for another time. Place stock in a saucepan. • Combine flour and milk and add to stock. Simmer for 10 minutes, stirring constantly. • Add chicken meat, potatoes, salsify and capers to sauce and reheat. Stir in sour cream and seasonings. • To serve, sprinkle with chopped chives.

Sweet and Sour Lentils
(top right photograph)

700 calories per serving
Preparation time: 10 minutes
Cooking time: 1 hour

| 1½ cups lentils |
| 6 cups water |
| 4 shallots |
| 1 large carrot |
| 1 lb. potatoes |
| 2 tbs. butter |
| 2 tbs. brown sugar |
| 3 smoked bratwurst sausages |
| ½ tsp. salt |
| 2 tbs. vinegar |

Wash and sort lentils. Drain. Place in a saucepan in water to cover and cook, uncovered, over low heat for 30 minutes. • Peel and dice shallots, carrots and potatoes. • Melt butter in a large saucepan. Add sugar and caramelize over low heat, stirring constantly. Add shallots and carrots and gently brown in the caramel. Pour in lentils and their cooking liquid. • Slice bratwurst and add to lentils with diced potatoes. Simmer for 30 minutes. • Season with salt and vinegar.

Green Peas with Bacon
(top left photograph)

640 calories per serving
Soaking time: 12 hours
Preparation time: 15 minutes
Cooking time: 2 hours

1¾ cups dried, green peas
8 cups water
1 lb. potatoes
2 leeks
½ lb. celeriac
½ tsp. dried summer savory
½ tsp. thyme
⅛ tsp. white pepper
1 tsp. salt
2 onions
6 strips bacon

Wash, sort and soak dried peas in water to cover for 12 hours. • Place peas and soaking water in a saucepan. Cover and simmer for 2 hours. • Peel, wash and dice potatoes. Wash leek and cut in half lengthwise; cut off dark green leaves and slice white parts. Peel, wash and finely dice celeriac. • Add potatoes, leeks, celeriac, summer savory, thyme, pepper and salt to peas the last ½ hour of cooking. • Peel onions and slice into rings. Chop bacon. • Fry bacon pieces until crisp. Remove from pan and drain on paper towels. Add onion rings to bacon fat and sauté until golden brown, turning constantly. • To serve, garnish with onion rings, bacon and chopped celeriac greens.

Navy Bean Stew
(bottom right photograph)

480 calories per serving
Soaking time: 12 hours
Preparation time: 10 minutes
Cooking time: 2 hours

1¾ cups dried, navy beans
6 cups water
2 large onions
3 cloves garlic
2 stalks of celery
2 large carrots
2 tbs. olive oil
1 tsp. salt
⅛ tsp. white pepper
⅛ tsp. dried marjoram
2 slices whole-wheat bread
2 tbs. margarine
1 tbs. chopped thyme
1 tbs. chopped parsley

Wash, sort and soak beans in 6 cups of water for 12 hours. • Place beans and soaking liquid in a saucepan, cover, and cook over low heat for 1½ hours. • Peel and dice onions and 2 garlic cloves. Slice celery. Scrape and dice carrots. • Heat olive oil in a frying pan. Add onions, diced garlic, celery and carrots and sauté for 5 minutes. Add sautéed vegetables to beans. • Season beans with salt, pepper and marjoram. Simmer, covered, 30 minutes longer. • Preheat oven to 450°F. • Chop remaining garlic clove, then crush it. Cut bread into 12 squares. Combine margarine, crushed garlic, thyme and parsley. Spread mixture on croutons. • Place croutons on cookie sheet and bake until crisp. To serve, spoon stew into a serving dish and top with croutons.

Salads and
Special Dishes

Mixed Salad

265 calories per serving
Preparation time: 20 minutes
Cooking time: 20 minutes

1 lb. celeriac
½ lb. cauliflower
4 small tomatoes
1 cucumber
4 small carrots
1 red pepper
1 onion
¼ lb. lamb's lettuce
¼ lb. radicchio
12 stuffed olives
⅛ tsp. coarsely ground black pepper
¼ cup olive oil
3 tbs. wine vinegar
½ tsp. salt
1 tbs. chopped, mixed fresh herbs
⅔ cup low-fat yogurt
1 hard-boiled egg

Wash celeriac. Place in boiling salt water to cover and cook, uncovered, for 25 minutes, or until tender. • Divide cauliflower into florets. Bring about 1 inch of water to a boil in a separate saucepan. Add cauliflower and simmer, partially covered, for 10 minutes. • Wash, dry and quarter tomatoes. Wash and slice cucumber. Scrape and grate carrots. Cut green pepper in half, remove seeds and inner membrane, and cut into julienne strips. Peel and slice onion into rings. Clean, wash and drain lamb's lettuce. Clean, wash and drain radicchio and divide into individual leaves. Cut olives in half. • Peel cooked celeriac and slice with a hors d'oeuvre cutter. Drain cauliflower florets. • Arrange all ingredients on a platter and sprinkle with pepper. Top with olives. • Stir olive oil, vinegar, salt, herbs and yogurt together until well blended. Pour dressing over salad in a thin stream. • Peel egg and cut into eighths. Garnish salad with egg wedges.

Wild Greens with Croutons

160 calories per serving
Preparation time: 30 minutes

½ lb. mixed wild greens
⅓ lb. Boston lettuce
1 small apple
1 tsp. maple syrup
1 tsp. lemon juice
3 tbs. walnut oil
1 tbs. cider vinegar
1 tbs. apple juice
⅛ tsp. salt
2 tbs. chopped chives
2 slices whole-wheat bread
1 clove garlic
2 tbs. margarine

Wash wild greens thoroughly; trim long stems and drain. Divide Boston lettuce into individual leaves; wash thoroughly and drain. Tear large leaves into pieces. Cut drained greens into smaller pieces and place in a salad bowl with Boston lettuce. • Quarter, peel, core and apple into julienne strips. Combine apple julienne with maple syrup, lemon juice, walnut oil, vinegar, apple juice and salt. Fold apple dressing and chopped chives into the salad. • Cut bread into ½-inch cubes. Peel, dice and crush garlic. Melt margarine in a frying pan. Add crushed garlic and bread cubes and sauté until croutons are golden. • To serve, sprinkle salad with croutons.

Spinach Salad

130 calories per serving
Preparation time: 20 minutes

1 lb. spinach leaves
2 oranges
1 apple
1 tbs. walnut oil
⅛ tsp. salt
½ tsp. ginger syrup
⅔ cup low-fat yogurt
¼ cup coarsely grated Jerusalem artichoke

Sort and thoroughly wash spinach leaves. Dry spinach, trim long stems and cut large leaves in half. • Peel 1 orange and divide into sections, removing seeds. Split open membrane with a sharp knife and lift out each section. Peel, core and thinly slice apple. Combine spinach leaves, orange sections and apple slices in a salad bowl. • Cut off a thin piece of rind from second orange and cut into julienne strips. Squeeze juice from orange. • Combine orange juice, walnut oil, salt, ginger syrup and yogurt and stir until well blended. Fold dressing the salad ingredients. • To serve, sprinkle salad with coarsely grated Jerusalem artichoke and orange rind julienne.

Tip: Grated coconut can be substituted for Jerusalem artichokes.

Asparagus Salad

205 calories per serving
Preparation time: 10 minutes
Cooking time: 20 to 30 minutes
Refrigeration time: 20 minutes

1 lb. asparagus
12 cups water
1 tsp. salt
½ tsp. sugar
3 tomatoes
3 hard-boiled eggs
¼ cup vegetable oil
2 tbs. cider vinegar
⅛ tsp. white pepper
2 tbs. chopped parsley

Peel asparagus from top to bottom, cut off woody ends and tie into 2 bundles. Combine water, ½ teaspoon of salt and sugar in a saucepan and bring to a boil. Add asparagus bundles and cook, covered, over low heat for 20 to 30 minutes. • Peel and quarter tomatoes. Cut tomato quarters into small cubes. • Remove asparagus bundles from pan, rinse with cold water, and drain. Remove string and cut asparagus spears into 2-inch pieces. • Peel eggs and cut into eighths. Arrange asparagus pieces, egg wedges and tomato cubes on a serving platter. Stir vegetable oil, vinegar, ½ teaspoon of salt and pepper until well blended. Pour dressing over salad in a thin stream. • Cover salad and refrigerate for 20 minutes. • To serve, sprinkle with chopped parsley.

Salade Niçoise

295 calories per serving
Preparation time: 20 minutes

1 small head bibb lettuce
1 lb. tomatoes
1 large onion
7 ozs. canned tuna
12 black olives
3 tbs. olive oil
1½ tbs. wine vinegar
½ tsp. salt
⅛ tsp. white pepper
2 hard-boiled eggs
1 tbs. chopped fresh basil

Wash lettuce well, dry and tear leaves into pieces. • Wash, dry and cut tomatoes into eighths. Peel and slice onions into thin rings. • Drain oil from tuna and divide tuna into 1-inch chunks. Combine tomato wedges, onion rings, tuna, lettuce and olives in a salad bowl and toss gently. • Mix olive oil, vinegar, salt and pepper together, stirring until well blended. Pour dressing over salad in a thin stream. • Peel eggs and cut into eighths.To serve, garnish salad with egg wedges and chopped basil.

Wax Bean Salad
(top left photograph)

175 calories per serving
Preparation time: 10 minutes
Cooking time: 15 minutes

1 lb. wax beans
1½ tsp. salt
2 sprigs of summer savory
¼ lb. shelled green peas
2 egg yolks
2 tbs. cider vinegar
2 tsp. prepared, mild mustard
⅛ tsp. white pepper
¼ cup vegetable oil

Wash and trim wax beans. Place in a saucepan with water to cover, 1 teaspoon of salt and summer savory and bring to a boil. Simmer, covered, for 15 minutes, or until tender. Drain. • Place peas in a separate saucepan in a small amount of boiling salt water. Boil gently for 5 to 10 minutes, then drain. • For the sauce, combine egg yolks, vinegar, mustard, ½ teaspoon of salt, pepper and olive oil. Stir until well blended. • Combine beans with peas while still warm. Pour in sauce and toss gently.

Green Bean Salad
(bottom left photograph)

215 calories per serving
Preparation time: 10 minutes
Cooking time: 10 minutes

1 lb. green beans
2 sprigs of summer savory
2 tsp. salt
2 green onions
2 hard-boiled eggs
3½ tbs. canned corn
2 tbs. sherry vinegar
¼ cup olive oil
2 tbs. finely chopped dill

Wash and trim beans. Place beans in a saucepan with water to cover, summer savory and 1 teaspoon of salt and bring to a boil. Cover and simmer for 10 minutes. Drain and set aside to cool. • Trim, wash and finely slice green onions. Peel and cut eggs into eighths. Drain corn. • Combine vinegar, 1 teaspoon of salt and olive oil and stir until well blended. Mix dressing, onions, corn and beans together in a serving dish. • To serve, arrange egg wedges on salad and sprinkle with dill.

Lima Bean Salad
(right photograph)

285 calories per serving
Preparation time: 10 minutes
Cooking time: 25 minutes
Refrigeration time: 1 hour

2¼ lbs. shelled lima beans
1½ tsp. salt
2 sprigs of summer savory
2 cloves garlic
2 tbs. cider vinegar
⅛ tsp. white pepper
⅓ cup walnut oil
5 fresh peppermint leaves

Place lima beans in a saucepan with water to cover, 1 teaspoon of salt, and summer savory. Bring to a boil, cover, and simmer for 25 minutes. • Drain beans and place in a serving bowl to cool. • Peel and finely chop garlic cloves. • Combine vinegar, remaining salt, garlic, pepper and walnut oil and stir until well blended. Cut peppermint leaves into julienne strips. Pour dressing over beans, add peppermint leaves and toss well. • Refrigerate salad, covered, for 1 hour.

Cucumber Salad

85 calories per serving
Preparation time: 10 minutes

| 2¼ lbs. cucumbers |
| 2⁄3 cup low-fat yogurt |
| ½ tsp. salt |
| ⅛ tsp. white pepper |
| 1 tbs. lemon juice |
| 2 tbs. maple syrup |
| Watercress for garnish |

Wash, dry and cut cucumbers in half lengthwise. Cut halves into ¼-inch slices. • Mix yogurt, salt, pepper, lemon juice and maple syrup together and fold into cucumbers. • To serve, garnish with watercress.

Tri-Colored Pepper Salad

230 calories per serving
Preparation time: 10 minutes

| 1 yellow pepper |
| 1 green pepper |
| 1 red pepper |
| 1 large onion |
| ¼ lb. feta cheese |
| 1 large clove garlic, crushed |
| ½ tsp. prepared mustard |
| ⅛ teaspoon salt |
| ⅛ teaspoon white pepper |
| ⅛ teaspoon sugar |
| 1 tbs. cider vinegar |
| 3 tbs. olive oil |
| 2 tbs. chopped parsley |

Wash peppers and cut in half. Remove membrane and seeds and cut into julienne strips. Peel and dice onion. Cut feta cheese into small cubes. • Peel and finely chop garlic clove. Mix garlic, mustard, salt, pepper, sugar, vinegar and olive oil together well. • To serve, combine pepper julienne, diced onion and feta cheese in a serving bowl and toss with dressing. Sprinkle with chopped parsley.

Tip: Two medium-sized, peeled and diced tomatoes can be substituted for the red pepper. Feta cheese can be replaced by ½ lb. of cooked, diced poultry.

Tomato Salad
(top photograph)

135 calories per serving
Preparation time: 10 minutes

6 medium-sized tomatoes
1 tsp. salt
2 shallots
3 tsp. chopped fresh basil
1 tbs. basil vinegar
⅛ tsp. black pepper
¼ cup olive oil

Wash, dry and slice tomatoes. Arrange on a serving platter and sprinkle with salt. • Peel and finely dice shallots. Sprinkle diced shallots and basil over tomatoes. • Mix vinegar, pepper and olive oil together well. To serve, pour dressing over tomatoes in a thin stream.

Tomato and Artichoke Heart Salad
(bottom photograph)

125 calories per serving
Preparation time: 15 minutes

4 medium-sized tomatoes
6 cooked artichoke hearts
2 green onions
1 tsp. salt
⅛ tsp. white pepper
2 tbs. tarragon vinegar
¼ cup olive oil

Peel and cut tomatoes into eighths. Drain artichoke hearts and cut into eighths. Wash and trim onions and slice into rings. Combine tomatoes, artichoke hearts and onions in a serving bowl. • Mix salt, pepper, vinegar and olive oil together well. To serve, toss salad with dressing.

Potato Salad with Herring Fillets
(left photograph)

315 calories per serving
Preparation time: 20 minutes
Cooking time: 12 to 15 minutes

1¾ lbs. red potatoes
½ lb. herring fillets marinated in sour cream
4 sweet gherkins
2 shallots
1 tbs. cider vinegar
1 tsp. lemon juice
½ tsp. salt
1 tbs. walnut oil
2 hard-boiled eggs

Wash potatoes. Place potatoes in a saucepan with boiling water to cover. Cover and boil gently for 12 to 15 minutes. Drain, cool, peel and slice potatoes. • Cut herring fillets into 1-inch wide strips. Dice sweet gherkins. Peel and dice shallots. Combine potatoes, sweet gherkins, shallots, herring strips and herring marinade in a serving bowl. • Mix vinegar, lemon juice, salt and walnut oil together well. Toss salad with dressing. • Peel eggs and cut into eighths. To serve, garnish salad with egg wedges.

Potato and Cucumber Salad
(right photograph)

205 calories per serving
Preparation time: 20 minutes
Cooking time: 25 to 30 minutes

1⅓ lbs. potatoes
1 lb. cucumbers
1 apple
1 large onion
1 tsp. salt
2 tbs. lemon juice
3 tbs. maple syrup
⅓ cup sour cream
3 tbs. chopped chives

Wash potatoes and place in a saucepan with salt water to cover. Bring to a boil, cover, and boil gently for 25 to 30 minutes. Drain, cool, peel and slice. • Wash, dry and thinly slice cucumbers. Peel, core and thinly slice apple. Peel and dice onion. • Combine potatoes, cucumbers and apples in a serving bowl. Mix salt, lemon juice, maple syrup and sour cream. To serve, toss salad with dressing and sprinkle with chopped chives.

Endive and Orange Salad
(left photograph)

110 calories per serving
Preparation time: 15 minutes

| 4 medium-sized heads endive |
| 1 orange |
| 2 hard-boiled eggs |
| 6 tbs. low-fat yogurt |
| 2 tbs. sour cream |
| ⅛ tsp. salt |
| ⅛ tsp. paprika |
| Watercress for garnish |

Trim and wash endive; drain and cut into julienne strips. Peel orange and divide into sections, removing seeds. Split open membrane with a sharp knife and lift out each section. Peel and dice eggs. Combine endive julienne, egg and orange sections in a serving bowl. • Mix yogurt, sour cream, salt and paprika together. Toss salad with dressing. • To serve, garnish with watercress.

Cauliflower Salad
(lower right photograph)

190 calories per serving
Preparation time: 20 minutes
Cooking time: 12 minutes

| 1 small head of cauliflower |
| 1 cup milk |
| 1 cup water |
| 3 tbs. cider vinegar |
| ½ tsp. herb salt |
| ⅛ tsp. white pepper |
| 1 tsp. honey |
| ½ tsp. prepared mustard |
| ¼ cup safflower oil |
| 1 tbs. chopped celery leaves |
| 2 tbs. chopped parsley |

Wash cauliflower, trim stalks and divide into florets. Place milk and water in a saucepan and bring to a boil. Add cauliflower, cover and simmer for 12 minutes. Drain and set aside in a serving bowl to cool. • Mix vinegar, herb salt, pepper, honey and mustard together. Add safflower oil. Toss cauliflower florets with dressing. Cover salad and set aside for 30 minutes. • To serve, cream sprinkle with celery leaves and chopped parsley.

Celery and Apple Salad
(top right photograph)

150 calories per serving
Preparation time: 15 minutes

| 1 lb. celery |
| 1 large red apple |
| 1 tbs. lemon juice |
| 1 tsp. prepared mustard |
| ½ tsp. salt |
| 1 tsp. ginger syrup |
| ½ cup whipping cream |

Wash and slice celery ribs. Core and thinly slice apple. • Mix lemon juice, mustard, salt and syrup together well. Place apple slices and celery in a serving bowl and toss with dressing. Whip cream until almost stiff. • To serve, place a dollop of whipped cream on top of salad and sprinkle with chopped celery leaves.

Carrot and Apple Salad

235 calories per serving
Preparation time: 30 minutes
Refrigeration time: 30 minutes

| 1⅓ lbs. carrots |
| ½ cup walnuts |
| ¾ cup low-fat yogurt |
| 2 tbs. lemon juice |
| ⅛ tsp. salt |

2 large apples

Scrape, wash and coarsely grate carrots. Peel, core and coarsely grate apples. Combine grated carrots and apples in a serving bowl and toss gently. • Coarsely chop walnuts, reserving 2 walnut halves for garnish. • Mix yogurt, lemon juice and salt together. Stir chopped walnuts into carrot and apple mixture. Spoon dressing on top of carrot and apple mixture. • Cover and refrigerate for 30 minutes. • To serve, garnish with walnut halves.

Tip: Whipping cream can be substituted for yogurt.

Carrot and Leek Salad

130 calories per serving
Preparation time: 20 minutes

| ⅔ lb. leeks |
| 1 lb. carrots |
| 1 large, tart apple |
| 1 bunch watercress |
| 1 tbs. lemon juice |
| 2 tbs. chopped fresh herbs, such as parsley, pimpernel and chives |
| ½ cup sour cream |
| ⅛ tsp. salt |

Trim dark leaves and stem ends from leeks. Cut stalks in half lengthwise, wash thoroughly, dry and slice thinly. Scrape, wash and cut carrots into julienne strips. Peel, core and coarsely grate apple. Wash watercress and drain well. • Arrange sliced leek, grated apple and carrot julienne on a serving platter. Sprinkle with lemon juice. • Mix herbs, sour cream and salt together. Pour dressing over salad and garnish with watercress.

Tip: Add julienned, cooked poultry for a light meal.

Avocado Salad

290 calories per serving
Preparation time: 10 minutes

2 avocados
1 red pepper
1 celery heart
½ onion
4 small sweet gherkins
7 tbs. ricotta or cottage cheese
1 egg yolk
2 tbs. vegetable oil
1 tbs. lemon juice
1 tsp. mustard
⅛ tsp. Worcestershire sauce
1 tsp. salt
⅛ tsp. white pepper
2 tbs. small capers

Peel avocados, remove seeds and slice. Cut red pepper in half, removing membrane and seeds; wash, dry and dice the pepper halves. Wash and thinly slice celery. Peel and dice onion. Dice sweet gherkins. • Combine ricotta or cottage cheese, egg yolk, vegetable oil, lemon juice, mustard, Worcestershire sauce, salt, pepper and capers, blending well. • Place avocado slices, red pepper, celery, onion and gherkins in a serving bowl. To serve, spoon dressing over salad.

Tip: Buy avocados a few days ahead of time. Underripe avocados usually require 2 to 3 days at room temperature to ripen. Enclosing avocados in a paper bag will hasten the ripening process.

Red Beet Salad

190 calories per serving
Preparation time: 20 minutes

1⅓ lbs. small red beets
2 large apples
2 small onions
2 tbs. lemon juice
1 tbs. molasses
⅛ tsp. salt
⅛ tsp. white pepper
⅛ tsp. ground caraway seeds
2 tbs. walnut oil

horoughly scrub red beets, peel and slice. Cut beets into julienne strips and place in a serving bowl. Peel, core and thinly slice apples. Peel and finely chop onions. • Mix lemon juice, molasses, salt, pepper and ground cara-way seeds together well. Add dressing, diced onions and sliced apples to beets. • To serve, sprinkle salad with walnut oil.

Tip: Add ¼ lb. grated celeriac and season dressing with 1 to 2 teaspoons of freshly grated horse-radish for a heartier taste.

Celery Salad

300 calories per serving
Preparation time: 20 minutes

1 lb. celery hearts
1 large, tart apple
2 tbs. lemon juice
3 slices fresh pineapple
½ cup shelled walnuts
1 tsp. salt
⅛ tsp. pepper
2 tbs. corn syrup
3 tbs. walnut oil

Wash celery heart ribs and cut into julienne slices. • Peel, core and finely dice apple. Sprinkle diced apple with lemon juice and mix with celery julienne.

• Peel pineapple slices, cut out woody cores and cut into chunks. Stir pineapple chunks into celery mixture. Place salad in serving bowl. • Combine salt, pepper, corn syrup and walnut oil, stirring well. Drizzle over salad. Chill well before serving.

Mushroom and Shrimp Salad

145 calories per serving
Preparation time: 15 minutes
Refrigeration time: 30 minutes

1 lb. mushrooms	
½ lb. fresh shrimp, cooked, peeled and deveined	
1 tbs. wine vinegar	
1 tbs. lemon juice	
3 tbs. walnut oil	
⅛ tsp. salt	
⅛ tsp. sugar	
⅛ tsp. white pepper	
2 tbs. sherry	
1 tbs. chopped parsley	
1 tbs. chopped chives	

Clean mushrooms, slice very thinly and place in a serving bowl. Rinse shrimp briefly, drain well, and add to mushrooms. • Mix wine vinegar, lemon juice, walnut oil, salt, sugar, white pepper and sherry together well. Toss mushrooms and shrimp with dressing. • Refrigerate salad, covered, for 30 minutes. • To serve, sprinkle salad with chopped herbs.

Tip: The shrimp may be replaced by finely diced smoked ham. For a milder dressing, substitute pineapple or apple juice for the vinegar.

Kohlrabi Salad

115 calories per serving
Preparation time: 10 minutes

2 large kohlrabies	
2 tbs. lemon juice	
1 celery heart	
1 large, tart apple	
¾ cup low-fat yogurt	
⅛ teaspoon salt	
⅛ teaspoon white pepper	
2 tsp. molasses	

Peel, wash and dry kohlrabies. Wash and finely chop the most tender leaves. Place leaves in a bowl, cover and set aside. Coarsely grate kohlrabies and mix with lemon juice. Trim, wash, dry and thinly slice celery heart. Peel, core and thinly slice apple. Combine celery, apple slices and kohlrabies in a serving bowl. • Blend yogurt, salt, pepper and molasses together well. Fold dressing into salad. To serve, sprinkle with chopped kohlrabi leaves.

Tip: Celery and apple may be replaced by 1 large cucumber. Cut kohlrabies and cucumber into julienne strips and replace kohlrabi leaves with chopped chives.

Chinese Cabbage Salad
(top left photograph)

125 calories per serving
Preparation time: 15 minutes

1⅓ lbs. Chinese cabbage	
1 small white radish	
1 red pepper	
1 small onion	
¼ cup grapefruit juice	
3 tbs. safflower oil	
1 tsp. prepared mustard	
⅛ tsp. salt	
½ tsp. ginger syrup	
2 tbs. chopped chives	

Trim cabbage, wash thoroughly, dry and cut into julienne strips. Peel, wash and coarsely grate radish. Cut red pepper in half, removing membrane and seeds; wash and finely dice pepper halves. • Peel and dice onion. • Mix grapefruit juice, safflower oil, mustard, salt and syrup together well. To serve, toss salad with dressing and garnish with chopped chives.

Chinese Cabbage and Bacon Salad
(top right photograph)

225 calories per serving
Preparation time: 20 minutes

1⅓ lbs. Chinese cabbage	
1 large onion	
½ tsp. salt	
⅛ tsp. black pepper	
3 tbs. cider vinegar	
2 tbs. apple juice	
3 tbs. safflower oil	
4 strips bacon	
2 tbs. chopped parsley	

Trim cabbage, wash thoroughly, dry and julienne. Peel and finely dice onion. Combine cabbage julienne and onion in a serving bowl. • Mix salt, pepper, vinegar, apple juice and safflower oil together well. Toss salad with dressing. • Finely dice bacon and sauté in a dry frying pan until crisp. Drain on paper towels. • To serve, fold diced bacon and bacon fat into salad and sprinkle with chopped parsley.

Chinese Cabbage Fruit Salad
(bottom right photograph)

80 calories per serving
Preparation time: 20 minutes

1⅓ lbs. Chinese cabbage	
2 kiwis	
2 oranges	
3 tbs. sour cream	
3 tbs. yogurt	
1 tbs. lemon juice	
⅛ tsp. salt	
⅛ tsp. pepper	
¼ cup watercress leaves	

Trim cabbage, wash thoroughly, dry and cut into julienne strips. Peel kiwis and oranges. Slice kiwis ¼–inch thick, then quarter the slices. Divide oranges into sections. Fillet oranges by splitting open membrane with a sharp knife and lifting out each section. Place cabbage, kiwis and oranges in a serving bowl. • Mix sour cream, yogurt, lemon juice, salt, pepper and watercress together well. Spoon dressing over salad.

Cabbage and Bacon Salad

430 calories per serving
Preparation time: 30 minutes
Marinating time: 1 hour

2¼ lbs. cabbage
8 cups water
2 tsp. salt
8 strips bacon
2 tsp. molasses
2 tsp. coarsely crushed caraway seeds
⅛ tsp. white pepper
2 to 3 tbs. wine vinegar
3 tbs. white wine
2 tbs. walnut oil

Trim cabbage, remove core and cut into julienne strips. Combine water and 1 teaspoon of salt in a saucepan and bring to a boil. Place cabbage julienne in a sieve and blanch in boiling water for 4 minutes. Remove and drain. • Finely dice bacon and sauté in a frying pan until crisp. • Mix 1 teaspoon of salt, molasses, crushed caraway seeds, white pepper, vinegar, white wine and walnut oil together well. • Mix well-drained cabbage julienne and dressing in a bowl. Add diced bacon to salad and toss gently. • Cover and set aside at room temperature for 1 hour.

Sauerkraut Salad

180 calories per serving
Preparation time: 10 minutes
Marinating time: 20 minutes

1¾ lbs. sauerkraut
1 large onion
1 large dill pickle
3 slices fresh pineapple
½ cup pineapple juice
¼ cup pickle juice
2 tbs. safflower oil

Gently toss sauerkraut with 2 forks in a large bowl. Peel and finely chop onions. Finely dice dill pickle. Peel pineapple slices, cut out woody cores and cut into chunks. • Mix pineapple juice, pickle juice and safflower oil together well. Add chopped onion, diced dill pickle, pineapple chunks and salad dressing to sauerkraut. • Cover salad and marinate for 20 minutes.

Tip: Add ⅔ cup of raisins for a sweeter salad. For a heartier salad, omit the pineapple, pineapple juice and safflower oil and add 7 ounces of tuna fish with the canned oil. For a more tart flavor, use 6 tablespoons of pickle juice and add cider vinegar to taste.

Red Cabbage and Fruit Salad

275 calories per serving
Preparation time: 30 minutes
Marinating time: 30 minutes

1½ lbs. red cabbage
8 cups water
1½ tsp. salt
⅓ cup cider vinegar
1 tbs. lemon juice
1 apple
1 large orange
1 banana
½ lb. fresh pineapple
3 tbs. walnut oil

Clean, trim and quarter cabbage. Remove core and cut into julienne strips. Bring water, 1 teaspoon of salt and 3 tablespoons of vinegar to a boil in a saucepan. Place cabbage julienne in a sieve and blanch in boiling water for 4 minutes; drain. Place cabbage in a large bowl. • Mix lemon juice, remaining vinegar and salt together well. Pour dressing over cabbage and mix well. • Peel, core and slice apple. Peel orange and divide into sections. Fillet orange by splitting open membrane with a sharp knife and lifting out each section. Peel banana, cut in half lengthwise and cut into slices. Peel pineapple and cut into chunks. Add fruit and walnut oil to red cabbage. • Cover and marinate at room temperature for 30 minutes.

Brussels Sprouts and Jerusalem Artichoke Salad

325 calories per serving
Preparation time: 10 minutes
Cooking time: 20 minutes

1¾ lbs. Brussels sprouts
1 tsp. salt
4 strips bacon
2 shallots
1¾ ozs. Jerusalem artichokes
2 tbs. safflower oil
2 tbs. white wine vinegar
6 tbs. vegetable stock
2 tbs. chopped parsley

Clean and trim Brussel sprouts and place in a saucepan. Sprinkle with salt and add water to cover. Bring to a boil. Simmer, uncovered, for 20 minutes, or until tender. Drain. Place in a serving bowl. • Dice bacon. Peel and finely dice shallots. Peel, wash and grate Jerusalem artichokes, then set aside. • Heat safflower oil in a frying pan. Add bacon and sauté until crisp, turning frequently. Remove from pan and drain. Sauté shallots in same pan until golden, stirring constantly. Remove from pan. • Combine white wine vinegar, vegetable stock, shallots, reserved bacon fat and Jerusalem artichokes with Brussels sprouts. To serve, sprinkle salad with diced bacon and chopped parsley.

Broccoli Salad with Turkey
(top left photograph)

285 calories per serving
Preparation time: 10 minutes
Cooking time: 12 minutes

1¾ lbs. broccoli
1 tsp. salt
1 onion
½ lb. turkey breast
¼ cup walnut oil
⅛ tsp. white pepper
2 tbs. white wine vinegar
¾ cup yogurt
8 whole, shelled walnuts

Trim, wash and divide broccoli into florets. Place enough water to cover broccoli and salt in a saucepan and bring to a boil. Add broccoli, cover, and simmer about 10 minutes, or until just tender. Drain and cool. • Peel and

dice onions. Cut turkey breast into 1-inch cubes. • Heat 2 tablespoons of walnut oil in a frying pan. Add diced onions and sauté until golden. Add diced turkey and sauté for about 4 minutes, stirring frequently. Season with salt to taste and pepper. • Combine remaining walnut oil with white wine vinegar and yogurt. Place broccoli, onions and turkey in a serving bowl. Spoon dressing on top. • To serve, coarsely chop walnuts and sprinkle over salad.

Broccoli Salad with Shrimp
(middle bottom photograph)

240 calories per serving
Preparation time: 10 minutes
Cooking time: 12 minutes

1¾ lbs. broccoli
1½ tsp. salt

1 large apple
⅛ tsp. white pepper
1 tsp. sugar
2 tbs. lemon juice
3 tbs. peach juice
¼ cup safflower oil
3½ ozs. cooked shrimp, shelled and deveined
2 tbs. chopped chives

Trim, wash and divide broccoli into florets. Place enough water to cover broccoli and 1 teaspoon of salt in a saucepan and bring to a boil. Add broccoli, cover, and simmer for 10 minutes, or until just tender. • Peel, core and cut apples into julienne strips. Stir apple julienne, ½ teaspoon of salt, pepper, sugar, lemon juice, peach juice and safflower oil together well. • To serve, place shrimp and broccoli in a serving bowl and toss with dressing.

Broccoli Salad with Grated Coconut
(right photograph)

295 calories per serving
Preparation time: 15 minutes
Cooking time: 12 minutes

1¾ lbs. broccoli
1 tsp. salt
3 hard-boiled eggs
1 onion
⅛ tsp. white pepper
⅛ teaspoon Tabasco sauce
¼ cup orange juice
¼ cup vegetable oil
⅔ cup grated coconut

Trim, wash and divide broccoli into florets. Trim and peel stems, then cut into 1-inch pieces. Sprinkle broccoli stems with salt and place in boiling water to cover. Cover and simmer for 6 minutes. Add florets and cook,

covered 6 minutes longer. Drain broccoli and place in a serving bowl to cool. • Peel and finely dice eggs. • Peel and grate onion. Combine grated onion, pepper, Tabasco sauce, orange juice and vegetable oil. • To serve, toss broccoli with dressing. Garnish with diced eggs and grated coconut.

Spinach with Wild Herbs

270 calories per serving
Preparation time: 1 hour

| ⅔ lbs. wild herb leaves |
| 1 lb. young spinach leaves |
| 16 cups water |
| 2 tsp. salt |
| 1 large onion |
| 2 cloves garlic |
| 2 tbs. safflower oil |
| 1 tsp. honey |
| ½ cup sour cream |
| 1 tbs. pine nuts |

Wash wild herbs and spinach, cutting off thick stems. • Combine water and salt in a saucepan and bring to a boil. Add wild herbs and spinach and blanch for 3 minutes. Drain and chop coarsely. • Peel and finely chop onion and garlic cloves. • Heat safflower oil in a saucepan and sauté chopped onion and garlic until transparent. Add the herbs and spinach and steam, covered, over low heat for 5 minutes. • Add salt to taste, honey and sour cream. Simmer liquid, uncovered, over low heat for five minutes to reduce. • To serve, sprinkle pine nuts over vegetables.

Creamed Swiss Chard

200 calories per serving
Preparation time: 20 minutes
Cooking time: 10 minutes

| 2¼ lbs. Swiss chard |
| 1 cup vegetable stock |
| 2 tsp. flour |
| 2 tbs. pineapple juice |
| ⅛ tsp. salt |
| ⅛ tsp. nutmeg |
| 2 tbs. almond paste |
| ⅛ teaspoon lemon juice |
| ½ cup whipping cream |

Wash Swiss chard thoroughly. Remove several green leaves and set aside in a covered bowl. • Shred remaining chard. Bring vegetable stock to a boil in a saucepan. Add chard and simmer, covered, for 10 minutes. • Blend flour and pineapple juice together well. Add to saucepan, stirring until sauce has thickened. Season chard with salt, nutmeg, almond paste and lemon juice. • Stir whipping cream into chard. Heat through. Transfer to a serving dish. • To serve, finely mince reserved leaves and sprinkle over cooked Swiss chard.

Snow Peas in Wine Sauce
(left photograph)

215 calories per serving
Preparation time: 15 minutes
Cooking time: 10 to 15 minutes

1½ lbs. sugar peas
2 tbs. butter
½ cup hot vegetable stock
3 egg yolks
1 tbs. cornstarch
⅛ tsp. salt
⅛ tsp. white pepper
½ cup dry white wine
⅛ teaspoon lemon juice
⅛ tsp. grated lemon rind
¼ cup whipping cream
3 egg whites
2 tbs. chopped dill

Wash, trim and drain snow peas. • Melt butter in a saucepan. Add peas and stir-fry for 3 minutes. Add hot vegetable stock and simmer, covered, for 10 to 15 minutes. Drain, reserving cooking liquid. • Whisk egg yolks, cornstarch, salt and pepper together in top of a double boiler. Simmer until thickened. Stir in white wine and season with lemon juice and rind. Combine sauce with whipping cream and reserved cooking liquid. • Beat egg whites until stiff and fold into sauce. • To serve, combine snow peas and sauce in a serving dish. Garnish with chopped dill.

Peas in Potato Wreaths
(right photograph)

380 calories per serving
Preparation time: 30 minutes
Cooking time: 35 to 40 minutes

1¾ lbs. potatoes
2 tsp. salt
1 lb. shelled peas
½ to 1 cup vegetable stock
5 tbs. butter
2 egg yolks
⅛ tsp. white pepper
⅛ tsp. nutmeg
1 egg yolk
2 tbs. milk
¼ cup freshly grated Swiss cheese
Oil for greasing

Peel, wash and dice potatoes. Place enough water to cover potatoes and 1 teaspoon of salt in a saucepan and bring to a boil. Add potatoes and boil gently for about 25 minutes. • Place peas, vegetable stock, ½ teaspoon of salt and sugar in a separate saucepan and bring to a boil. Simmer, covered, for 20 minutes. • Drain cooked potatoes, cool, and mash. • Preheat oven to 400°F. Grease a baking sheet with oil. • Mix ½ teaspoon of salt, pepper and nutmeg into mashed potatoes. Place potato mixture in pastry tube and press out 8 equal-sized wreaths. Whisk egg yolk and milk together and brush on potato wreaths. • Drain peas and spoon into center of potato wreaths. Sprinkle each portion with grated cheese and dot with butter. • Place on middle rack of oven and bake for 10 to 15 minutes.

Lima Beans with Béchamel Sauce
(left photograph)

290 calories per serving
Preparation time: 15 minutes
Cooking time: 1 hour

3⅓ lbs. lima beans
2 cups vegetable stock
2 sprigs of summer savory
2 tbs. butter
1 tbs. flour
1 small onion
½ bay leaf
2 cloves
⅛ tsp. salt
⅛ tsp. pepper
⅛ tsp. nutmeg
½ cup whipping cream
1 tsp. anchovy paste
2 tbs. chopped parsley

Shell lima beans, rinse with cold water and drain. Place vegetable stock and summer savory in a saucepan and bring to a boil. Add beans and simmer, covered, for 30 minutes. Drain beans, reserving 1½ cups of cooking liquid. • Melt butter in a saucepan. Add flour and sauté until golden, stirring constantly. Add reserving cooking liquid, continuing to stir. • Peel onion, stick with bay leaf and cloves and add prepared onion to sauce. Simmer sauce for 30 minutes, stirring frequently. • Remove onion. Season sauce with salt, pepper and nutmeg. Stir whipping cream and anchovy paste together and mix into sauce. • To serve, place lima beans in a serving dish and mix with sauce. Garnish with chopped parsley.

Green Beans with Sour Cream
(right photograph)

185 calories per serving
Preparation time: 20 minutes
Cooking time: 10 to 20 minutes

1¾ lbs. green beans
1 onion
1 clove garlic
2 medium-sized carrots
2 tbs. vegetable oil
½ cup hot vegetable stock
2 sprigs of summer savory
1 tsp. cornstarch
¼ cup sour cream
2 tsp. chopped thyme

Trim and wash green beans. Halve or quarter longer beans. Peel and dice onion.

Finely chop garlic. Scrape, wash and cut carrots into small cubes. • Heat vegetable oil in a saucepan. Add onion and garlic and sauté, stirring constantly. Add beans and carrots and stir-fry briefly. Add vegetable stock and summer savory. Simmer vegetables for 15 minutes. Remove vegetables from pan and place in serving dish. • Mix cornstarch with a little cold water, then add to cooking liquid, stirring until sauce has thickened. Mix vegetables with sauce and serve garnished with chopped thyme and sour cream.

Kohlrabies and Carrots
(top left photograph)

285 calories per serving
Preparation time: 30 minutes
Cooking time: 20 to 25 minutes

3 kohlrabies
2 large carrots
4 medium-sized potatoes
2 small onions
2 strips bacon
2 cups meat stock
⅛ tsp. salt
⅛ tsp. paprika
2 tbs. chopped watercress

Peel and dice kohlrabies, carrots, potatoes and onions. Cut bacon into small cubes. Wash and finely chop tender kohlrabi leaves. Cover and set aside for garnish. • Sauté bacon in a saucepan until crisp. Remove from pan and drain. • Add onion to same pan and sauté until transparent. Add remaining vegetables and stir-fry briefly. Pour in meat stock and simmer, covered, for 20 to 25 minutes. • To serve, season with salt and paprika and garnish with watercress, kohlrabi leaves and diced bacon.

Creamed Kohlrabi
(bottom photograph)

235 calories per serving
Preparation time: 10 minutes
Cooking time: 10 to 15 minutes

4 kohlrabies
3 tbs. vegetable oil
½ cup hot vegetable stock
½ cup whipping cream
⅛ tsp. salt
⅛ tsp. pepper
2 tbs. chopped parsley

Peel and cut kohlrabi into ¼-inch slices. Wash and chop tender kohlrabi leaves and set aside in a covered bowl. • Heat vegetable oil in a large frying pan. Add kohlrabi slices and sauté for 3 minutes. Pour in vegetable stock and simmer for 10 to 15 minutes. • Add whipping cream to kohlrabi slices and season with salt and pepper. Transfer to a serving dish, sprinkle with chopped parsley and reserved kohlrabi leaves. Serve hot.

Kohlrabi with Ham
(top right photograph)

360 calories per serving
Preparation time: 15 minutes
Cooking time: 20 minutes

5 kohlrabies
3 tbs. butter
1 cup hot meat stock
1 sprig of lovage
⅛ tsp. sugar
⅛ tsp. salt
⅛ tsp. black pepper
⅛ tsp. nutmeg
3½ ozs. lean, cooked ham
2 strips bacon
1 tsp. lovage

Peel kohlrabies, slice thinly, then quarter. Wash and finely chop tender kohlrabi leaves and set aside in a covered bowl. • Melt butter in a saucepan. Add kohlrabi slices and sauté for 3 minutes. Add stock, lovage, sugar, salt, pepper and nutmeg. Simmer, covered, over low heat for 20 minutes. • Cut ham into 1-inch strips and fold into kohlrabi mixture. • Sauté bacon in a frying pan until crisp. Remove from pan and drain. • To serve, sprinkle kohlrabi with chopped lovage and reserved kohlrabi leaves. Lay bacon slices on top.

Eggplant with Tomato Sauce

420 calories per serving
Preparation and marinating time: 40 minutes
Cooking time: 40 minutes

2¼ lbs. small eggplants	
2 tsp. salt	
1 onion	
2 cloves garlic	
6 tomatoes	
¼ cup plus 1 tsp. flour	
½ cup olive oil	
1 tsp. chopped rosemary	
⅛ tsp. white pepper	
1 tbs. cider vinegar	

Thinly peel eggplants, cut lengthwise into ½-inch slices and sprinkle with salt. Cover and set aside for 30 minutes. • Peel and chop onion and garlic cloves. Peel tomatoes and cut into eighths. • Pour liquid off eggplants and blot dry. Coat eggplant slices with ¼ cup flour. • Heat olive oil in a frying pan. Fry eggplant slices on both sides until golden brown. Remove from pan, drain and keep warm. • Pour off half the olive oil. Sauté chopped onion and garlic in remaining oil until golden. Add tomatoes and sauté for 2 minutes. Add rosemary, salt to taste and pepper and simmer, covered, for 5 minutes. • Combine remaining flour and vinegar. Add to tomato sauce, stirring until sauce has thickened. Simmer for 5 minutes. Serve tomato sauce as an accompaniment to eggplant slices.

Zucchini Stew

325 calories per serving
Preparation time: 30 minutes
Cooking time: 20 minutes

1¾ lbs. small zucchini	
2 cloves garlic	
1 tsp. salt	
⅛ tsp. black pepper	
4 strips bacon	
½ cup hot vegetable stock	
1 tbs. chopped sage	
6 tbs. whipping cream	
⅛ tsp. paprika	
2 tbs. chopped chives	

Wash, dry and cut zucchini into 1-inch cubes. Peel and dice garlic cloves, sprinkle with salt and pepper and crush with a fork. Combine zucchini cubes and crushed garlic in a bowl. • Dice bacon and sauté in a frying pan until crisp. Remove bacon from pan and drain. • Sauté zucchini on all sides in same frying pan. Add vegetable stock and sage. Cover and simmer for 15 minutes. • Combine whipping cream and paprika and mix into zucchini. Simmer, uncovered, over low heat to heat through. • To serve, sprinkle zucchini with diced bacon and chopped chives.

Tip: ½ lb. of cooked, lean ham, cubed or ½ lb. of cooked, diced poultry can be substituted for the bacon. This will reduce the calorie count by about 100 calories per serving.

Glazed Carrots
(top photograph)

185 calories per serving
Preparation time: 20 minutes
Cooking time: 20 minutes

1¾ lbs. carrots
3 tbs. safflower oil
1 tbs. maple syrup
½ cup vegetable stock
2 tsp. cornstarch
3 tbs. whipping cream
⅛ tsp. salt
1 tbs. chopped peppermint

Scrub carrots and cut into ½-inch cubes. • Heat safflower oil in a saucepan and stir in maple syrup. Add carrots and stir-fry for 5 minutes. Pour in vegetable stock. Simmer, covered, for 20 minutes, adding additional vegetable stock if necessary. • Blend cornstarch and whipping cream together well. Add to carrots, stirring until cooking liquid has thickened. To serve, season carrots with salt and sprinkle with chopped peppermint.

Carrots in Wine Sauce
(bottom photograph)

180 calories per serving
Preparation time: 10 minutes
Cooking time: 20 To 30 minutes

1¾ lbs. carrots
3 tbs. butter
½ cup sweet white wine
½ tsp. salt
2 tbs. chopped parsley

Scrape, wash and slice carrots. • Melt butter in a saucepan. Add carrots and stir-fry for 5 minutes. Add wine and salt, mixing well. • Simmer carrots, covered, for 20 to 30 minutes. • To serve, sprinkle with chopped parsley.

Fennel with a Cheese Crust
(bottom photograph)

265 calories per serving
Preparation time: 20 minutes
Cooking time: 50 minutes

1¾ lbs. fennel
1 tsp. salt
3 tbs. butter
2 tbs. flour
½ cup warm milk
⅛ tsp. white pepper
⅛ tsp. nutmeg
¼ cup freshly grated Parmesan cheese
Butter for greasing

Trim, wash and quarter fennel bulbs. Chop tender fennel greens and set aside for garnish. • Place fennel bulbs in a saucepan, sprinkle with salt and add water to cover. Bring to a boil. Cover and simmer for 40 minutes. • Preheat oven to 450° F. Grease an oven-proof dish. • Drain cooked fennel bulbs, reserving ½ cup of cooking liquid. • Melt half the butter in a saucepan. Add flour and sauté until golden, stirring constantly. Pour in reserved cooking liquid. Add milk simmer for 5 minutes, stirring constantly. Season with salt to taste, pepper and nutmeg. • Place fennel and reserved chopped greens in a buttered serving dish and cover with sauce. Sprinkle with Parmesan cheese and dot with butter. Bake for 10 minutes.

Celery with a Cheese Crust
(top photograph)

Trim 2¼ lbs. of celery and cut into 2½-inch pieces. Place in a saucepan with salted water to cover and bring to a boil. Simmer, covered, for 30 minutes. Chop tender celery leaves and set aside. • Place celery in an ovenproof dish and bake in the Béchamel sauce as described in the recipe above. Serve sprinkled with reserved celery leaves.

Sweet-and-Sour Cucumbers

140 calories per serving
Preparation time: 15 minutes
Cooking time: 20 minutes

2¼ lbs. cucumbers	
2 tbs. margarine	
1 tsp. prepared mustard	
½ tsp. salt	
1 tsp. maple syrup	
2 tbs. lemon juice	
½ cup hot vegetable stock	
1 egg yolk	
6 tbs. whipping cream	
2 tbs. finely chopped dill	

Peel and halve cucumbers; remove seeds and cut into ¼-inch slices. • Melt margarine in a saucepan. Add cucumber slices and stir-fry for 1 minute. Mix in prepared mustard, salt, maple syrup and lemon juice. Pour in vegetable stock, cover pan and simmer for 20 minutes. • Uncover pan after 20 minutes and continue simmering for 3 minutes to reduce liquid. Remove vegetables from heat. • Whisk egg yolk and cream together. Fold 2 tablespoons of hot cooking liquid into egg yolk mixture. Add mixture to vegetables, stirring constantly, until cooking liquid has thickened. • To serve, adjust seasonings and sprinkle with chopped dill.

Tip: For a thicker sauce, combine 1 to 2 teaspoons of cornstarch with a small quantity of cold water. Stir mixture into vegetables and boil for 3 minutes, stirring constantly. Remove from heat and stir in the egg yolk and cream mixture.

Turnips in Port Sauce

145 calories per serving
Preparation time: 30 minutes
Cooking time: 20 minutes

1¾ lbs. turnips	
1 tsp. salt	
3 tbs. butter	
2 tbs. flour	
2 tbs. sugar	
⅓ cup port wine	

Peel, wash, dry and dice turnips. Place diced turnips, salt and water to cover in a saucepan and bring to a boil. Boil gently for about 20 minutes. Drain, reserving 2 cups of cooking liquid. • Melt 2 tablespoons butter in a large saucepan. Add flour and sauté until golden, stirring constantly. Gradually pour in reserved cooking liquid, stirring vigorously with a whisk. Boil sauce for 5 minutes. • Add diced turnips to sauce. • Heat remaining butter in a small saucepan, add sugar and cook until caramelized, stirring constantly. Stir in wine and pour over turnips. • Simmer turnips for 5 minutes.

Tip: Turnips are also tasty in a Béchamel sauce. Substitute milk for half the cooking liquid and season with salt, a pinch of white pepper and nutmeg. Omit caramelized sugar and sprinkle with 3 to 4 tablespoons of chopped chives.

Creamed Cauliflower

255 calories per serving
Preparation time: 35 minutes
Cooking time: 30 to 35 minutes

2¼ lbs. cauliflower
2 cups milk
2 cups water
3 tbs. butter
1 tbs. flour
½ cup whipping cream
2 egg yolks
½ tsp. salt
⅛ tsp. nutmeg
2 tbs. chopped chives

Trim green leaves and stem from cauliflower, and score a deep cross into core. • Combine milk and water in a saucepan and bring to a boil. Place cauliflower,

head up, in mixture. Cover and cook for 20 to 25 minutes, or until tender. • Drain cauliflower, reserving 1 cup of cooking liquid. Divide cauliflower into florets and keep warm. • Melt butter in a saucepan. Add flour and sauté until golden, stirring constantly. Gradually stir in reserved cooking liquid and simmer sauce gently for 10 minutes, stirring constantly. • Whisk whipping cream, egg yolks, salt and nutmeg together. Stir 2 tablespoons of hot sauce into whipping cream mixture. Remove sauce from heat and combine with egg yolk and whipping cream mixture. Add cauliflower florets to sauce and heat through, without boiling. • To serve, sprinkle cauliflower with chopped chives.

Glazed Sweet Potatoes

380 calories per serving
Preparation time: 15 minutes
Cooking time: 30 minutes

1¾ lbs. sweet potatoes
1 tsp. salt
½ cup maple syrup
1 tsp. angostura bitters
1 tsp. lemon juice
3 tbs. butter

Scrub sweet potatoes under cold, running water. Place in a saucepan in boiling water to cover and cook, covered, over low heat for 30 minutes. Drain sweet potatoes and let cool. Peel, quarter and sprinkle with salt. •

Heat maple syrup, angostura bitters, lemon juice and butter in a saucepan, stirring constantly. • Before serving, glaze sweet potatoes by heating them in syrup over very low heat, turning frequently.

Baked Celery
(top left photograph)

230 calories per serving
Preparation time: 40 minutes
Cooking time: 50 minutes

4½ lbs. celery	
4 cups water	
1⅛ tsp. salt	
3 tbs. vinegar	
1½ cups vegetable stock	
3 shallots	
2 tbs. margarine	
1 tbs. flour	
2 eggs, separated	
½ cup freshly grated Swiss cheese	

Remove celery ribs, wash thoroughly and strip off leaves. Trim ends and coarse edges and cut ribs into 2-inch pieces. • Combine water, 1 teaspoon of salt and vinegar in a saucepan and bring to a boil. Add celery pieces and blanch for 5 minutes. • Drain, cool slightly and pull off strings. • Place vegetable stock in a saucepan and bring to a boil. Add celery pieces and cook, covered, over low heat for 30 minutes. Drain, reserving stock, and set aside. • Peel and dice shallots. • Melt margarine in a saucepan. Add shallots and sauté until transparent. Add flour and sauté until golden. Gradually pour in vegetable stock and simmer for 5 minutes, stirring constantly. Remove sauce from heat • Preheat oven to 450°F. Grease an ovenproof dish with margarine. • Fold egg yolks into sauce. Combine egg whites and ⅛ teaspoon of salt and beat until stiff. Fold egg whites into sauce. • Place celery pieces in ovenproof dish, cover with sauce and sprinkle with grated cheese. • Bake for 20 minutes.

Swiss Chard with Buttered Bread Crumbs
(bottom right photograph)

215 calories per serving
Preparation time: 10 minutes
Cooking time: 15 to 20 minutes

3⅓ lbs. Swiss chard	
6 cups water	
2 tsp. salt	
1 onion	
¼ cup butter	
⅓ cup bread crumbs	

Wash and dry Swiss chard and strip leaves from stalks. Remove strings and leaves from stalks and thick ribs. Cut stalks and ribs into 2-inch pieces. • Combine water and salt in a saucepan and bring to a boil. Add stalks and ribs and cook for 15 to 20 minutes. • Peel and dice onions. Coarsely chop the most tender chard leaves. • Melt 1 tablespoon of butter in a saucepan. Add onions and sauté until transparent. Add chopped chard leaves and steam, covered, over low heat for 5 minutes. • Melt remaining butter in a frying pan and sauté bread crumbs until golden brown. • To serve, drain chard stalks and ribs and transfer to a warmed serving platter. Sprinkle with sautéed leaves and buttered bread crumbs.

Fried Endive

410 calories per serving
Preparation time: 20 minutes
Cooking time: 10 minutes

8 small-sized heads endive
2 lemons
8 cups water
3 tsp. salt
⅔ cup flour
2 eggs, separated
½ cup light beer
1 tsp. sugar
1 cup parsley
4 cups vegetable oil

Trim endives and remove core. Squeeze juice from lemons. • Combine water, 2 teaspoons of salt and lemon juice in a saucepan and bring to a boil. Add endives and boil for 10 minutes. Drain and set aside to cool. • Sift flour into a bowl. Add egg yolks, beer, remaining salt and sugar to flour. • Heat vegetable oil in a deep-fat fryer to 350°F. • Beat egg whites until stiff and fold into batter. Wash and dry parsley. • Dip each endive in batter until completely coated. Fry a few at a time in hot oil until crispy and brown, turning frequently. Remove from oil and drain on paper towels. Return oil temperature to 350°F after each batch. • Transfer fried endive to a warm serving platter and keep warm. Fry parsley for 2 to 3 minutes in the hot fat and drain briefly. To serve, garnish endive with fried parsley.

Parsnip Pancakes

325 calories per serving
Preparation time: 10 minutes
Cooking time: 1 hour

1⅓ lbs. parsnips	
½ cup vegetable stock	
½ cup wheat germ	
2 eggs	
1 tbs. dried yeast	
½ tsp. salt	
2 tbs. chopped parsley	
⅓ cup safflower oil	

Peel parsnips, wash thoroughly, dry and cut into slices. Place vegetable stock in a saucepan and bring to a boil. Add parsnips and simmer for 40 minutes, adding additional stock or water if necessary. • Slightly cool parsnips and cooking liquid, then puree cooked parsnips and cooking liquid in a blender or food processor. Sprinkle wheat germ over puree. Add eggs, dried yeast, salt and chopped parsley and mix into a smooth dough. With damp hands, shape dough into 4- to 5-inch cakes. • Heat safflower oil in a frying pan. Fry pancakes on both sides until golden. Drain and transfer to a serving platter. Keep warm until all pancakes are made. Serve hot.

Tip: Cooked parsnips can also be deep-fried using the batter in the preceding recipe for Fried Endive.

Jerusalem Artichoke Fritters

355 calories per serving
Preparation time: 30 minutes
Cooking time: 30 minutes

1⅓ lbs. Jerusalem artichokes	
1½ tsp. salt	
4 cups water	
½ red pepper	
⅔ cup wheat germ	
1 tbs. paprika	
2 eggs, separated	
⅓ cup safflower oil	

Wash, peel and slice Jerusalem artichokes. Bring water and 1 teaspoon salt to a boil in a saucepan. Add sliced Jerusalem artichokes and cook, covered, over low heat for 15 to 20 minutes. • Wash pepper, remove seeds and membrane and chop finely. • Place wheat germ in a bowl. Add remaining salt, paprika and chopped pepper and mix well. Add egg yolks to wheat germ mixture. Drain Jerusalem artichokes, dice finely and mix into batter. Beat egg whites until stiff. • Heat safflower oil in a frying pan. Pour in 1 tablespoon of batter per fritter and spread out slightly with a spatula. Brown fritters on both sides until crispy. Drain and transfer to a serving platter. Keep finished fritters warm until all batter is used.

Creamed Celeriac
(top photograph)

150 calories per serving
Preparation time: 10 minutes
Cooking time: 30 minutes

1¾ lbs. celeriac
2 tbs. margarine
1 cup hot water
1 tsp. salt
½ tsp. light molasses
⅛ tsp. white pepper
1 tbs. flour
½ cup hot vegetable stock
¼ tsp. herb salt
1 egg yolk
¼ cup sour cream

Trim greens from celeriac and set aside. Scrub celeriac bulb, peel, rinse again and cut into thick slices. Dice celeriac slices. • Melt margarine in a saucepan. Add diced celeriac and sauté until lighter in color. Add water, salt, light molasses and pepper. Simmer, covered, for about 25 minutes, or until tender. • Dust celeriac with flour and add vegetable stock and herb salt. Bring to a boil, then simmer 5 minutes longer. • Wash and finely chop reserved celeriac greens. Whisk egg yolk and sour cream together. • Remove celeriac from heat and add egg yolk mixture, stirring until cooking liquid has thickened. • To serve, sprinkle with chopped celeriac greens.

Sliced Celeriac with Beef Marrow
(bottom photograph)

225 calories per serving
Preparation time: 10 minutes
Cooking time: 20 minutes

1 large celeriac
Juice of 1 lemon
1 tsp. sugar
1 tsp. salt
2 large onions
3 tbs. butter
2 large beef marrow bones
¼ tsp. coarsely grated black pepper
2 tbs. chopped parsley

Scrub celeriac under running water. Peel, rinse again and cut into slices. Place celeriac, lemon juice, sugar, salt and water to cover in a saucepan and bring to a boil. Boil gently, uncovered, for 20 minutes. Drain and set aside. • Finely chop tender celeriac leaves, cover and set aside. • Peel and chop onions. Melt butter in a frying pan. Add onions and sauté until browned. • Place marrow bones in a saucepan in rapidly boiling water to cover for 3 minutes. Drain and press marrow out of bones. Cut marrow in half diagonally. • To serve, arrange celeriac slices on 4 plates. Top with a layer of onion mixture and a piece of marrow. Season marrow with salt to taste and pepper and garnish with chopped parsley and celeriac greens.

Kohlrabi Puree
(left top photograph)

125 calories per serving
Preparation time: 15 minutes
Cooking time: 25 minutes

1¾ lbs. kohlrabies
1 large onion
1 clove garlic
1 cup vegetable stock
¼ cup chopped watercress
1 tbs. butter
¼ cup whipping cream
⅛ tsp. salt
⅛ tsp. nutmeg

Peel and dice kohlrabies. Wash most tender kohlrabi leaves, chop coarsely and set aside. • Peel and finely dice onion and garlic cloves. Combine diced kohlrabi, onion, garlic and vegetable stock in a saucepan and bring to a boil. Boil gently, uncovered, for 25 minutes. • Add chopped watercress and kohlrabi leaves during last 5 minutes of cooking time. • Cool slightly, then puree kohlrabi and cooking liquid in a blender or food processor. Return to saucepan and simmer, stirring constantly, until liquid is slightly reduced. • To serve, add butter and whipping cream. Season with salt and nutmeg.

To make Pureed Celeriac
(right top photograph)

Trim, scrub and dice 2¼ lbs. celeriac. Sprinkle with 1 tablespoon lemon juice. Dice 1 onion. Place celeriac, onion and 1 cup of vegetable stock in a saucepan and bring to a boil. Boil gently for 20 minutes, or until celeriac is tender. Puree celeriac, cooking liquid, 6 tablespoons whipping cream, ½ teaspoon salt and white pepper in a blender or food processor. Garnish with sautéed onion rings.

Pureed Lentils
(middle top photograph)

285 calories per serving
Preparation time: 20 minutes
Cooking time: 1 hour, 30 minutes

1⅓ cups lentils
1 bunch of soup greens
1 onion
4 cups water
½ bay leaf
1 tbs. butter
2 tbs. whipping cream
⅛ tsp. salt
⅛ tsp. white pepper

Wash and sort lentils; drain. Trim soup greens. Peel and quarter onion. Place lentils in a saucepan in water and bring to a boil. Add soup greens, onion and bay leaf. Simmer, covered, for 1½ hours. • Cool slightly, then puree lentils in a blender or food processor. Return puree to saucepan and simmer, stirring constantly, until puree is smooth. • To serve, stir in butter and cream and season to taste with salt and pepper.

Pureed Green Peas
(bottom left on plate)

285 calories per serving
Preparation time: 10 minutes
Cooking time: 20 minutes

3⅓ lbs. unshelled green peas
1½ cups water
1 tsp. salt
1 tsp. sugar
1 sprig of fresh dill
1 sprig of fresh chervil
1 sprig of parsley
6 tbs. whipping cream
2 tbs. butter

Shell peas. Place peas, water, salt, sugar and herbs in a saucepan and bring to a boil. Cover and simmer for 20 minutes. • Remove herbs. Puree peas and their cooking liquid in a blender or food processor. Stir in whipping cream and butter.

Glazed Turnips

130 calories per serving
Preparation time: 15 minutes
Cooking time: 35 minutes

1¾ lbs. young turnips	
3 tbs. butter	
2 tbs. sugar	
1 cup hot vegetable stock	
¼ tsp. salt	
⅛ tsp. white pepper	
1 tsp. cornstarch	
2 tbs. whipping cream	
2 tbs. chopped parsley	

Scrub turnips. Peel, rinse again and dry. Leave small turnips whole, cut larger ones in halves or quarters. • Melt butter in a large saucepan. Add sugar, stirring constantly, and cook until slightly brown. Add turnips and stir-fry in browned sugar until turnips are light brown. • Pour in hot vegetable stock and simmer, covered, for 30 minutes. Season with salt and pepper. Mix cornstarch and whipping cream together, stirring until cornstarch is dissolved. Add cornstarch mixture to turnips, stirring constantly until cooking liquid has thickened. • Transfer turnips to a warmed serving dish and sprinkle with parsley.

Broccoli with Buttered Bread Crumbs

275 calories per serving
Preparation time: 15 minutes
Cooking time: 15 minutes

2¼ lbs. broccoli	
½ cup vegetable stock	
½ cup dry white wine	
1 tsp. salt	
3 tbs. butter	
1 cup dry bread crumbs	

Wash, dry and trim broccoli. Thinly peel stalks from top to bottom and divide into florets. • Place vegetable stock, wine and salt in a saucepan and bring to a boil. Add broccoli stalks and simmer for 5 minutes. Add broccoli florets and simmer 10 minutes longer. • Melt butter in a small saucepan. Add bread crumbs and sauté until golden brown. To serve, sprinkle broccoli with bread crumbs.

Tip: The bread crumb topping may be replaced by ½ cup of whipping cream combined with 1 cup of freshly grated cheese. Pour mixture over broccoli and bake in a preheated 450°F oven for about 10 minutes.

Brussels Sprouts with Chestnuts

435 calories per serving
Preparation time: 20 minutes
Cooking time: 20 minutes

1¾ lbs. Brussels sprouts
10 cups water
1 tsp. salt
1 lb. chestnuts
3 tbs. butter
2 tbs. honey
1 cup hot vegetable stock
⅛ tsp. nutmeg

Trim and wash Brussels sprouts. • Bring 6 cups of water and 1 teaspoon of salt to a boil in a saucepan. Add Brussels sprouts and cook, covered, over low heat for 20 minutes. • Bring 2 cups of water to a boil in a separate saucepan. Score pointed end of chestnuts with a deep cross. Place chestnuts in boiling water and cook, covered, over high heat for 20 minutes. • Drain Brussels sprouts. • Drain chestnuts; peel and pull off inner skin. • Heat butter and honey in a saucepan, stirring constantly. Add chestnuts, turning frequently. Pour in hot vegetable stock and steam, covered, over low heat for 10 minutes. • Add Brussels sprouts to chestnuts and heat through over very low heat. Season with salt to taste and nutmeg.

Steamed Caraway Cabbage
(top photograph)

300 calories per serving
Preparation time: 15 minutes
Cooking time: 40 minutes

2¼ lbs. cabbage
7 tbs. clarified butter
2 tsp. brown sugar
½ cup hot vegetable stock
2 tsp. caraway seeds
½ tsp. salt

Trim cabbage. Quarter head, cut out core and separate individual leaves. Cut leaves into 2-inch strips. • Melt clarified butter in a large saucepan. Add brown sugar, stirring until sugar is melted. Fold cabbage strips into butter in portions and sauté for 2 minutes before adding next portion. Gradually pour in hot vegetable stock. Add caraway seeds and steam cabbage, covered, over low heat for 40 minutes, adding more stock or water if necessary. • To serve, transfer to a serving dish and season with salt.

Tip: Instead of adding caraway seeds, use 4 tsp. brown sugar and season with freshly grated ginger and soy sauce. Thicken sauce with 1 to 2 tablespoons of cornstarch dissolved in wine vinegar.

Savoy Cabbage with Bacon
(bottom photograph)

215 calories per serving
Preparation time: 10 minutes
Cooking time: 25 minutes

2¼ lbs. savoy cabbage
8 cups water
1 tsp. salt
1 cup hot vegetable stock
¼ cup sour cream
2 tsp. green peppercorns
4 slices bacon

Wash and trim savoy cabbage and cut into quarters. • Bring water and salt to a boil in a saucepan. Add cabbage and blanch for 10 minutes. • Preheat oven to 450°F. • Drain cabbage quarters and arrange in an ovenproof dish. Pour in hot vegetable stock. Combine the sour cream with green peppercorns and spread over cabbage quarters. • Bake for 15 minutes. • Sauté bacon in a frying pan until crisp. Remove from pan and drain. • To serve, garnish cabbage with bacon slices.

Red Cabbage with Apples
(left photograph)

180 calories per serving
Preparation time: 20 minutes
Cooking time: 1 hour

2¼ lbs. red cabbage	
2 tart apples	
2 tbs. clarified butter	
½ cup hot vegetable stock	
1 tsp. salt	
3 cloves	
3 tbs. red wine vinegar	
2 tbs. red currant jelly	

Wash and trim red cabbage. Quarter head, remove core and cut into julienne strips. Peel, core and slice apples. • Melt clarified butter in a saucepan. Add cabbage julienne and stir-fry for 5 minutes. Add hot vegetable stock, salt and cloves. Simmer, covered, for 1 hour, adding more stock or water if necessary. • Add apples and vinegar after 30 minutes of cooking. • To serve, add red currant jelly and season to taste with salt and red wine vinegar.

Champagne Sauerkraut
(right photograph)

340 calories per serving
Preparation time: 10 minutes
Cooking time: 50 minutes

2¼ lbs. sauerkraut	
1 large onion	
1 bay leaf	
2 cloves	
3½ ozs. salt pork	
2 tbs. vegetable oil	
½ cup hot meat stock	
½ cup dry white wine	
⅛ tsp. salt	
⅛ tsp. sugar	
½ cup champagne	

Toss sauerkraut with 2 forks. Peel onion and stick it with bay leaf and cloves. Cut salt pork into 4 uniform pieces. • Heat vegetable oil in a saucepan. Add sauerkraut and stir-fry briefly. Add hot meat stock, prepared onion, salt pork and white wine. Cook, covered, over medium heat for 50 minutes. • Remove salt pork and onion. Season sauerkraut with salt and sugar. • To serve, add champagne to sauerkraut and mix well.

Tip: For a milder taste, omit the salt pork. Cook sauerkraut with the prepared onion. Add ½ to ⅔ pound fresh crushed pineapple 10 minutes before the end of the cooking period. To serve, add champagne.

International Specialties

Russian Borscht

435 calories per serving
Preparation time: 10 minutes
Cooking time: 1 hour, 30 minutes

6 cups water
1 tsp. salt
⅛ tsp. black pepper
1 lb. beef neck bones
3½ ozs. lean salt pork
1 lb. cabbage
1 lb. red beets
1 tbs. red wine vinegar
1 parsnip
¼ celeriac
1 large onion
1 small leek
½ cup sour cream
1 tbs. chopped parsley

Place water, salt and pepper in a stock pot and bring to a boil. Wash salt pork and beef bones and place in rapidly boiling water. Repeatedly skim scum that rises to the surface during first 30 minutes of cooking time. • Trim cabbage. Cut cabbage into quarters, remove core and cut into julienne strips. • Peel and wash beets. Set aside 1 beet and cut rest into julienne strips. Grate reserved beet and combine with vinegar. • Peel or scrape parsnip and celeriac, wash and dice finely. Peel and dice onion. Trim, wash and slice white part of leek. • Add cabbage and beet julienne, parsnip, celeriac, onion and leek to stock pot after 40 minutes of cooking. Continue cooking, covered, for 50 minutes longer. • Remove meat from soup and cut into cubes. Stir grated beet and meat cubes into soup. • To serve, place sour cream on top of soup and sprinkle with parsley.

Provençal Soup

275 calories per serving
Preparation time: 30 minutes
Cooking time: 30 minutes

2 leeks
2 onions
1 lb. potatoes
4 large tomatoes
2 cloves garlic
1 fennel
3 tbs. olive oil
3 cups hot vegetable stock
½ tsp. salt
⅛ tsp. cayenne
1 tbs. chopped parsley

Trim dark green leaves and root end from leeks. Cut leeks in half lengthwise, wash and slice thinly. Peel and dice onions. Peel, wash and slice potatoes. Peel and dice tomatoes. Peel and crush garlic cloves. Trim fennel and cut into julienne strips. • Heat olive oil in a large saucepan and sauté diced onions and leek slices. Add potatoes, tomatoes, crushed garlic, fennel and vegetable stock and bring to a boil. Simmer for 30 minutes. • Cool slightly, then puree vegetables and cooking liquid in a blender or food processor. Season with salt and cayenne. • To serve, garnish with parsley.

Tip: In France, well-buttered, toasted slices of French bread, sprinkled with parsley, are floated on the surface of the soup just before serving.

Andalusian Gazpacho

365 calories per serving
Preparation time: 15 minutes
Refrigeration time: 2 hours

| 1 lb. tomatoes |
| 2 onions |
| 2 large cloves garlic |
| 1 cucumber |
| 1 large green pepper |
| 2 cups water |
| 2 tbs. wine vinegar |
| 2 tbs. olive oil |
| 3 tbs. bread crumbs |
| 1 tbs. tomato paste |
| 1 tsp. salt |
| ⅛ tsp. black pepper |
| ⅛ tsp. sugar |
| 6 slices stale white bread |
| 2 tbs. butter |
| 1 large onion |

Peel tomatoes and cut into eighths. Peel and coarsely chop onions and garlic cloves. Wash and dry cucumber and pepper. Coarsely dice half of the cucumber. Cut pepper in half, remove membrane and seeds and dice. Puree prepared vegetables in a blender or food processor. Whisk vegetable puree, water, vinegar, olive oil, bread crumbs and tomato paste together. Season with salt, pepper and sugar. • Refrigerate for 2 hours. • Dice bread. Melt butter in a frying pan. Add bread cubes and sauté until brown,. Remove from pan and set aside to cool. • Peel and finely chop onion. Cut remaining cucumber into small cubes. • To serve, arrange croutons, chopped onion and cucumber cubes on a small serving platter and serve with the chilled soup.

Bulgarian Cucumber Soup

285 calories per serving
Preparation time: 10 minutes
Resting time: 2 hours

| 3 cloves garlic |
| 1 tsp. salt |
| ¼ cup olive oil |
| 2¼ lbs. cucumbers |
| 2 cups yogurt |
| ½ cup sour cream |
| ⅛ tsp. white pepper |
| ¼ cup finely chopped fresh dill |
| 2 tbs. ground hazelnuts |

Peel and dice garlic, sprinkle with salt and crush. Stir olive oil into garlic a spoonful at a time. • Peel and grate cucumbers. Stir cucumbers, yogurt, sour cream and garlic mixture together. Season with salt to taste and white pepper. Refrigerate, covered, for at least 2 hours. • To serve, place 2 ice cubes in each soup cup, ladle in soup and sprinkle with chopped dill and ground hazelnuts.

Tip: Low-fat yogurt can be substituted for whole-milk yogurt. The cucumbers can be replaced by 2¼ lbs. tomatoes. Steam tomatoes in ¼ cup olive oil, without garlic. Puree in a blender or food processor. Return to saucepan. Dissolve 2 teaspoons of cornstarch in a little cold water and add to tomato puree, stirring constantly. Bring to a boil. Cool and combine with yogurt and sour cream.

Finnish Vegetable Stew
(top photograph)

380 calories per serving
Preparation time: 30 minutes
Cooking time: 20 minutes

5 cups water	
1½ tsp. salt	
1 small cauliflower	
2 large carrots	
1 lb. potatoes	
½ lb. green beans	
5 radishes	
½ lb. shelled peas	
½ lb. spinach	
2 tbs. flour	
2 tbs. softened butter	
⅛ tsp. sugar	
⅛ tsp. white pepper	
1 lb. cooked shrimp, peeled and deveined	
⅓ cup whipping cream	
2 tbs. chopped fresh dill	

Combine water and 1 teaspoon of salt in a saucepan and bring to a boil. • Remove outer green leaves from cauliflower. Divide into florets, wash and drain. Scrape and dice carrots. Peel, wash and dice potatoes. Wash, trim and cut green beans into pieces. Wash and quarter radishes. • Place prepared vegetables in a large saucepan in boiling water to cover. Boil gently, covered, for 15 minutes. • Wash, sort and coarsely chop spinach. Add to vegetables and cook for 5 minutes. Drain vegetables, reserving cooking liquid. Set aside. • Mix flour and butter together, shaping into a ball. Stir ball into reserved cooking liquid until dissolved. Boil for 5 minutes. Season sauce with ½ teaspoon of salt, sugar and pepper. Add shrimp and simmer until heated through. Add vegetables and reheat. • To serve, add whipping cream and sprinkle with chopped dill.

Béarnaise Vegetable Stew
(bottom photograph)

290 calories per serving
Preparation time: 10 minutes
Cooking time: 1 hour, 10 minutes

6 cups water	
1⅛ tsp. salt	
1 lb. fresh beef brisket	
½ onion	
1 bay leaf	
1 lb. potatoes	
1 large carrot	
4 turnips	
½ lb. cabbage	
½ lb. green beans	
1 parsnip	
1 sprig of lovage	
2 sprigs of chervil	
⅛ tsp. white pepper	
1 tbs. chopped parsley	

Combine water and salt in a large saucepan and bring to a boil. Add beef, onion and bay leaf. Boil gently, uncovered, for 30 minutes, frequently skimming scum that rises to surface. • Peel and dice potatoes, carrot and turnips. Shred cabbage and cut beans into pieces. Scrape, peel and dice parsnip. • Add prepared vegetables, lovage and chervil to meat after 30 minutes of cooking and simmer 40 minutes. • Remove meat from pan, dice and return to stew. • To serve, season to taste and sprinkle with parsley.

Alsatian Sauerkraut
(left photograph)

655 calories per serving
Serves: 8
Preparation time: 10 minutes
Cooking time: 2 hours

4½ lbs. sauerkraut
1 onion
1 bay leaf
2 cloves
1 clove garlic
5 juniper berries
2 cups dry Alsatian white wine
1½ cups water
¼ cup goose fat
½ tsp. salt
8 small potatoes
½ lb. bacon
1⅓ lbs. smoked boneless ham
8 knackwurst

Wash sauerkraut in lukewarm water. Squeeze out excess water and place sauerkraut in a large saucepan. • Peel onion and stick it with bay leaf and cloves. Peel garlic clove. Add prepared onion, garlic, juniper berries and wine to sauerkraut. Pour in water. Stir in goose fat and salt. Simmer, covered, for 2 hours, stirring occasionally. • Peel and wash potatoes. Add to sauerkraut after 1½ hours of cooking. • Place bacon, ham and knackwurst in a separate saucepan in boiling water to cover. Simmer for 30 minutes. • Remove onion and garlic clove from sauerkraut. Spoon sauerkraut into a serving dish and place potatoes on top. Slice pork, cut knackwurst in half and arrange on top of sauerkraut and potatoes.

Hungarian Cabbage Casserole
(right photograph)

600 calories per serving
Preparation time: 20 minutes
Cooking time: 40 minutes

½ cup long-grain rice
4½ cups water
2 tsp. salt
1¾ lbs. cabbage
1 small onion
1 lb. ground pork sausage
1 egg
⅛ tsp. paprika
2 tbs. pork fat
1 lb. sauerkraut
2 tbs. tomato paste

Wash rice. Combine 4 cups of water and 1 teaspoon of salt in a saucepan and bring to a boil. Add washed rice, cover and simmer for 15 minutes. Drain. •

Remove 12 large leaves from cabbage, setting remainder aside to use in another recipe. • Bring a large quantity of salt water to a boil in a separate saucepan. Add cabbage leaves and blanch for 5 minutes. Drain and flatten leaves. • Peel and dice onion. • Combine pork sausage, diced onion, egg, 1 teaspoon of salt, paprika and drained rice. • Make 4 cabbage rolls by laying 3 cabbage leaves on top of each other. Place a quarter of the sausage mixture in center of top leaf. Roll up leaves, tie with kitchen twine and fasten with wooden toothpicks. • Preheat oven to 400°F. • Melt pork fat in an ovenproof dish. Add stuffed cabbage rolls and brown on all sides. Remove cabbage rolls and set aside. Place sauerkraut in same ovenproof dish. • Combine tomato paste and ½ cup of water and mix with sauerkraut. Place stuffed cabbage rolls on top and bake for 40 minutes.

Ratatouille

395 calories per serving
Preparation time: 50 minutes
Cooking time; 45 minutes

| 1 medium-sized eggplant |
| 2 tsp. salt |
| 1 lb. zucchini |
| 2 onions |
| 2 red peppers |
| 1 yellow pepper |
| 4 large tomatoes |
| ⅔ cup olive oil |
| 3 cloves garlic |
| ½ tsp. ground coriander |
| 1 tsp. chopped fresh basil |
| ⅛ tsp. black pepper |
| ½ to 1 cup vegetable stock |
| 1 tbs. chopped parsley |

Cut eggplant into ½-inch slices. Place slices on a plate an sprinkle with salt. Place

another plate on top. Set aside for 30 minutes. Drain eggplant slices. • Wash and slice zucchini. Peel and dice onions. Wash peppers, remove membrane and seeds and cut into julienne strips. Peel and dice tomatoes. • Heat a quarter of the olive oil in a frying pan. Add eggplant slices and sauté, but do not brown. Drain and set aside. Add more olive oil and repeat procedure, first with zucchini, then with onions, and finally with yellow pepper. • Peel and finely dice garlic cloves. Combine sautéed vegetables, garlic, coriander, basil, salt to taste and pepper in a large saucepan or stew pot. Pour in 1 inch of vegetable stock. Cook vegetables, covered, over low heat for 30 minutes. • Add tomatoes and parsley and cook 15 minutes longer.

Hungarian Goulash

255 calories per serving
Preparation time: 20 minutes
Cooking time: 30 minutes

| 1 lb. tomatoes |
| ½ lb. green peppers |
| ½ lb. yellow peppers |
| 2 large onions |
| 4 strips bacon |
| 1 tbs. paprika |
| ½ tsp. salt |
| ⅛ tsp. black pepper |

Peel and dice tomatoes. Wash peppers and cut in half, removing membrane and seeds. Chop halves into pieces. • Peel and slice onions, then cut slices in quarters. • Dice bacon and sauté in a frying pan until crisp. Remove bacon from pan and drain. Sauté onions in same frying

pan until golden. Add peppers and stir-fry for 5 minutes. • Add tomatoes, paprika, salt and pepper. Cook, covered, over low heat for 30 minutes.

Oriental Stir-fried Vegetables

240 calories per serving
Preparation time: 40 minutes
Cooking time: 15 minutes

8 dried Chinese mushrooms
2 cups hot water
4 green onions
⅔ lb. celery
⅔ lb. carrots
⅔ lb. red peppers
⅓ lb. bamboo shoots
⅓ lb. bean sprouts
1 small clove garlic
1 small piece of fresh ginger
⅓ cup peanut oil
¼ cup soy sauce
½ tsp. salt
⅛ tsp. sugar
⅛ tsp. black pepper

Soak dried mushrooms in hot water for 30 minutes. • Trim, wash and cut green onions, celery and carrots into juliene strips. Wash peppers and cut peppers in half, removing membrane and seeds. Cut peppers into julienne strips. Drain bean sprouts. Drain and slice bamboo shoots. Peel, finely dice and crush garlic clove. Peel and grate ginger. • Heat peanut oil in a wok or large frying pan. Add garlic, ginger and onion and stir-fry for 1 minute. • Measure out ½ cup of the soaking liquid from mushrooms and set aside. Squeeze out mushrooms and cut in quarters. • Add celery, carrots and mushrooms to onion mixture and stir-fry for 4 minutes. • Pour in reserved mushroom liquid. Add peppers and stir-fry for 6 minutes. • To serve, season with soy sauce, salt, sugar and pepper. Add bamboo shoots and bean sprouts and stir-fry 3 minutes longer.

Neapolitan Vegetable Casserole
(top photograph)

535 calories per serving
Preparation time: 40 minutes
Cooking time: 40 to 50 minutes

1 lb. eggplant
3 tsp. salt
2 yellow peppers
4 large tomatoes
1⅓ lbs. potatoes
2 large onions
2 cloves garlic
½ cup olive oil
4 fresh basil leaves
⅛ tsp. black pepper
2 tbs. chopped chives

Thinly peel eggplant and cut into 1-inch thick strips. Sprinkle with 2 teaspoons of salt and set aside, covered, for 30 minutes. • Wash peppers, removing membrane and seeds and cut into julienne strips. Peel tomatoes and chop. Peel potatoes and cut into 1- inch cubes. Peel onions and slice. Peel and finely chop garlic cloves. • Preheat oven to 400°F. • Heat olive oil in an ovenproof dish with a cover. Add onions and garlic and sauté until onions are transparent. Add prepared vegetables. Mince basil leaves and stir into vegetables with 1 teaspoon of salt and pepper. • Cover dish and bake vegetables for 40 to 50 minutes. • To serve, sprinkle with chopped chives.

Swiss Onions au Gratin
(bottom photograph)

465 calories per serving
Preparation time: 15 minutes
Cooking time: 55 minutes

1⅓ lbs. potatoes
1⅓ lbs. onions
1 tsp. salt
½ tsp. coarsely grated black pepper
1 cup vegetable stock
½ cup whipping cream
1½ cups freshly grated Gruyère cheese
3 tbs. butter
1 tbs. chopped parsley

Preheat oven to 400°F. • Peel and slice potatoes and onions. Fill an ovenproof dish with alternating layers of potatoes and onions. Sprinkle each layer with salt and pepper. Pour in vegetable stock. • Bake casserole for 40 minutes. • Mix whipping cream and grated cheese together and spread over vegetables. Dot with butter on top and bake for 15 minutes longer, or until golden brown. • To serve, sprinkle with parsley.

Endive Casserole
(top photograph)

490 calories per serving
Preparation time: 30 minutes
Cooking time: 25 minutes

4 heads endive	
6 cups water	
1½ tsp. salt	
1 tbs. lemon juice	
1 lb. boneless chicken breasts	
3 tbs. butter	
1 tbs. flour	
1 cup hot poultry stock	
½ cup whipping cream	
⅛ tsp. nutmeg	
⅛ tsp. white pepper	
4 slices lean, cooked ham	
2 egg yolks	
¼ cup grated Gouda cheese	

Trim root ends from endive. Combine water, 1 teaspoon of salt and lemon juice in a saucepan and bring to a boil. Add endive and simmer for 15 minutes. Remove from pan and set aside. • Finely dice chicken breasts. Melt 2 tablespoons of butter in a frying pan. Add diced chicken and sauté for 6 minutes, turning frequently. • Combine 1 tablespoon of butter, flour and poultry stock in a separate saucepan, stirring constantly. Simmer sauce for 10 minutes. • Stir whipping cream, nutmeg, ½ teaspoon of salt, pepper and chicken meat into sauce. • Preheat oven to 400°F. • Cut endive in half. Fill 4 of the halves with chicken mixture. Place remaining 4 halves on top of filled halves and wrap each halve in a slice of ham. Place stuffed endive in an ovenproof dish. • Combine remaining chicken mixture with egg yolks and grated cheese and pour over endive. • Bake for 10 minutes.

Italian Zucchini Casserole
(bottom photograph)

350 calories per serving
Preparation time: 30 minutes
Cooking time: 30 to 35 minutes

4 medium-sized zucchini	
6 cups water	
3 tsp. salt	
2 yellow peppers	
4 tomatoes	
2 cloves garlic	
3 sprigs of fresh basil	
8 anchovy fillets	
3 tbs. olive oil	
⅓ lb. thinly sliced Mozzarella cheese	

Wash and dry zucchini. Trim and discard stem ends and cut in half lengthwise. • Preheat broiler • Combine water and 2 teaspoons of salt in a saucepan and bring to a boil. Add zucchini halves and blanch for 5 minutes. Drain and place in an ovenproof dish. Sprinkle with ½ teaspoon of salt. • Roast peppers on all sides in broiler. Pull off skin and cut in half, removing membranes and seeds. Cut peppers into julienne strips. • Peel tomatoes and cut into pieces. Arrange vegetables in an ovenproof casserole. • Peel and finely chop garlic cloves. Wash and dry basil and mince leaves. Cut anchovy fillets in half lengthwise. • Preheat oven to 400°F. • Heat 2 tablespoons olive oil in a large frying pan with lid. Add garlic, basil and vegetables and sauté for 1 minute. Season with ½ teaspoon of salt and simmer, covered, for 10 minutes. Pour the mixture over zucchini. Place anchovy strips on top and cover with Mozzarella cheese. Sprinkle with 1 tablespoon olive oil. • Bake for 20 to 25 minutes.

Chili con Carne

405 calories per serving
Serves: 6
Soaking time: 12 hours
Preparation time: 20 minutes
Cooking time: 1 hour, 30 minutes

1¾ cups dried kidney beans
2 onions
2 cloves garlic
3 tbs. vegetable oil
1 lb. ground beef
2 tsp. salt
¼ tsp. black pepper
1 tsp. cayenne
1 dried chili pepper, crushed
1 tbs. paprika
1 cup tomato juice

Wash and sort beans, cover with fresh water and soak for 12 hours. • Peel and finely chop onions and garlic cloves. Sauté onions and garlic in vegetable oil until golden. Add ground beef and brown slightly. • Combine meat, beans, soaking liquid, salt, pepper, cayenne, crushed chili pepper, paprika and tomato juice in a large saucepan. Simmer, uncovered, for 1½ hours, stirring frequently and adding additional tomato juice if necessary.

Tip: For a quick meal, use a 1 lb. can of kidney beans. The dish will be done after 20 minutes of cooking. If desired, 3 or 4 peeled and diced tomatoes can be added 10 minutes before the end of the cooking period.

Moussaka

550 calories per serving
Serves: 6
Preparation time: 30 minutes
Cooking time: 1 hour, 10 minutes

2 onions	
5 tomatoes	
2 cloves garlic	
1 lb. eggplant	
4 tbs. butter	
½ lb. ground beef	
½ lb. ground pork	
1 cup dry white wine	
2 tbs. chopped parsley	
1 tsp. salt	
1 tsp. white pepper	
½ tsp. dried thyme	
½ tsp. dried rosemary	
2 tbs. olive oil	
¼ tbs. flour	
3 cups warm milk	
½ cup freshly grated Gruyère cheese	

Peel and chop onions. Peel and dice tomatoes. Slice 1 tomato thinly. Peel and finely chop garlic cloves. Wash and slice eggplant lengthwise. • Melt 1 tablespoon of butter in a large saucepan. Add onions and sauté until transparent. Add ground meats and brown slightly. Add white wine, diced tomatoes, parsley, ½ teaspoon of salt, ½ teaspoon of pepper, thyme, rosemary and garlic. Simmer, covered, for 40 minutes. • Heat olive oil in a frying pan. Add eggplant slices and sauté until browned. Remove from pan and drain. • Preheat oven to 400°F. • Melt 3 tablespoons of butter in a small saucepan. Add flour, stirring constantly. Stir in milk, ½ teaspoon of salt and ½ teaspoon of pepper. Simmer sauce for 10 minutes. • Arrange alternating layers of eggplant slices, ground meat and sauce in an ovenproof dish, reserving ½ cup of sauce. Finish with a top layer of eggplant. Layer tomato slices down the middle. Pour a thin stream of sauce on top and sprinkle with grated cheese. • Bake for about 30 minutes.

Pan-Fried Eggplant

320 calories per serving
Preparation time: 45 minutes
Cooking time: 50 minutes

1⅓ lbs. small eggplants	
3½ tsp. salt	
3 onions	
1 clove garlic	
2 tomatoes	
1 lb. boneless veal shoulder roast	
1 tbs. butter	
3 tbs. peanut oil	
¼ tsp. coarsely grated pepper	
2 cups hot meat stock	

Wash and slice eggplants. Sprinkle with 3 teaspoons of salt and set aside for 30 minutes. • Peel and dice onions and garlic. Crush diced garlic. Peel and dice tomatoes. Cut veal into 1-inch cubes. • Rinse eggplant slices with cold water and blot dry. • Heat butter and peanut oil in a large frying pan. Add eggplant slices and sauté until light brown. Drain on paper towels. • Sauté diced onion in same pan until transparent. Add veal cubes and sauté until crisp and brown. Add garlic, tomatoes, ½ teaspoon of salt and pepper. • Pour in hot meat stock. Simmer, covered, for 30 minutes. Add eggplant slices and simmer 20 minutes. • Serve with boiled rice.

Onion Flan

345 calories per serving
Serves: 15
Preparation time: 1 hour, 30 minutes
Baking time: 40 minutes

For the dough:

3¼ cups flour

2 pkgs. dried yeast

⅛ tsp. sugar

⅔ cup plus 2 tbs. lukewarm milk

3 tbs. butter, flaked

½ tsp. salt

For the filling:

3⅓ lbs. onions

1 clove garlic

1 tsp. salt

½ lb. bacon

¼ cup vegetable oil

½ cup dry white wine

⅛ tsp. white pepper

½ tsp. crushed caraway seeds

1 tsp. dried rosemary

3 eggs

3 tbs. sour cream

2 tbs. bread crumbs

1½ cups freshly grated Swiss cheese

Sift flour into a bowl and make a depression in the middle. Add yeast. Sprinkle sugar over yeast and pour in lukewarm milk. Mix yeast with flour and milk. Dust with a little flour, cover and set aside to rise for 15 minutes. • Distribute flakes of butter around edge of flour and sprinkle with salt. Knead dough in bowl until it no longer sticks to bowl. Cover and set aside in a warm place to rise for 30 minutes, until dough doubles in volume. • Peel and thinly slice onions into rings. Peel and dice garlic. Sprinkle garlic with 1 teaspoon of salt and crush with a fork. Finely dice bacon. •

Heat vegetable oil in a large saucepan. Add onions and sauté until transparent, stirring constantly. Pour wine over onions. Add pepper, crushed caraway seeds, rosemary and crushed garlic. Cover and simmer for 20 minutes. • Sauté bacon in a frying pan until crisp. Remove from pan and drain. • Grease a baking sheet. • Roll out yeast dough to size of baking sheet, place on baking sheet and let rise again for 20 minutes. • Preheat oven to 400°F. • Whisk eggs, sour cream and bread crumbs together. Stir egg mixture into onions. Spread onion mixture onto dough, sprinkle with sautéed bacon and top with grated cheese. • Bake for 40 minutes. Cut flan into serving pieces while still hot and serve warm.

Tip: Prepare the following dough for an Alsatian onion flan: Knead 3¼ cups flour, ¾ cup plus 2 tablespoons of butter, 1 teaspoon salt, 1 egg and enough water to make a pliable dough. Season onion mixture with salt, pepper and grated nutmeg. Use 4 strips of bacon and mix eggs with 7 tablespoons of sour cream.

Celery Quiche

190 calories per serving
Serves: 12
Preparation time: 30 minutes
Baking time: 40 minutes

For the dough:
1⅔ cups flour
¼ cup vegetable shortening
⅛ tsp. salt
½ cup water
For the filling:
1½ lbs. celery
2 cups water
½ tsp. salt
2 medium-sized onions
4 eggs
3 tbs. whipping cream
¾ to 1 cup freshly grated Parmesan cheese
⅛ tsp. white pepper
⅛ tsp. nutmeg

Grease a 10½-inch spring-form pan. • Combine flour, vegetable shortening, salt and water to make a smooth dough. Spread dough out in springform pan to cover bottom and sides. Refrigerate. • Trim and wash celery. Cut celery in half lengthwise, then cut into small pieces. Bring water and salt to a boil in a sauce-pan. Add celery, cover and boil gently for 8 minutes. Drain. • Peel and finely dice onions. • Preheat oven to 450°F. • Whisk eggs and whipping cream together. Stir in celery, onions and Parmesan cheese. Season with white pepper, nutmeg and salt to taste. Remove springform pan from refrigerator and spoon filling into shell. • Bake on middle oven rack for 40 minutes. Serve hot.

Spanikopita

280 calories per serving
Serves: 10
Preparation time: 1 hour
Baking time: 50 minutes

1 10 oz. package frozen puff pastry
2¼ lbs. spinach
4 cups water
1 tsp. salt
5 green onions
1 clove garlic
3 tbs. butter
⅛ tsp. white pepper
⅛ tsp. nutmeg
½ lb. feta cheese
4 eggs
⅓ cup bread crumbs
1 egg yolk

Thaw puff pastry. • Sort and wash spinach. Bring water and salt to a boil in a saucepan. Add spinach and blanch for 4 minutes. Drain and chop coarsely. • Peel and finely dice green onions and garlic. Melt butter in a large frying pan. Add onions or shallots and garlic and sauté until transparent. Add spinach and sea-son with salt to taste, pepper and nutmeg. • Crumble feta cheese. Whisk eggs and mix with bread crumbs and crumbled feta cheese. • Preheat oven to 400°F. • Rinse a baking sheet with cold water. • Roll out puff pastry very thinly, then cut 6 rectangles mea-suring 10 x 12 inches. Arrange 3 rectangles on half of a baking sheet so that some of the pastry hangs over edges of pan. Spread spinach mixture on top of pastry rectangles and fold in the edges. Lay remaining puff pastry rectan-gles on top of spinach. Pierce pas-try repeatedly with a fork. Brush top of puff pastry with slightly beaten egg yolk and bake for 50 minutes, or until pastry is golden.

Leek Quiche

410 calories per serving
Serves: 10
Preparation time: 15 minutes
Refrigeration time: 1 hour
Baking time: 45 minutes

For the dough:
2 cups flour
7 tbs. butter
⅛ tsp. salt
1 egg
For the topping:
1⅓ lbs. leeks
½ lb. bacon
1 tbs. vegetable oil
¼ tsp. salt
¼ tsp. black pepper
⅛ tsp. curry
½ lb. ham
2 eggs
1 cup sour cream

Sift flour into a bowl. Dice butter. Add salt, egg and diced butter to flour and knead well. Cover and refrigerate for 1 hour. • Wash leeks and cut in half lengthwise. Trim and discard dark green leaves and root ends. Cut white parts of leeks into slices. • Dice bacon. Heat vegetable oil in a frying pan. Add bacon and sauté until crisp. Add sliced leeks and season with ⅛ teaspoon of salt, ⅛ teaspoon of pepper and curry. Simmer, covered, for 10 minutes. • Preheat oven to 400°F. • Remove dough from refrigerator and roll out. Line bottom and sides of a 10½-inch springform pan with rolled-out dough. Repeatedly pierce bottom with a fork. Dice ham and arrange on bottom of pastry shell. Place leek filling on top. Whisk eggs, sour cream and remaining salt and pepper together. Pour mixture over leek filling. • Bake for 45 minutes. Serve warm.

Tomato Quiche

205 calories per serving
Serves: 8
Preparation time: 40 minutes
Baking time: 33 minutes

1-7 oz. package frozen puff pastry
1⅓ lbs. tomatoes
3 eggs
⅛ tsp. salt
⅛ tsp. white pepper
½ tsp. chopped fresh basil
⅓ cup sour cream
1 tbs. melted butter
⅓ cup freshly grated Gruyère cheese

Thaw puff pastry and roll out on a floured work surface. Rinse a quiche pan with cold water. Line bottom and sides of pan with puff pastry. • Preheat the oven to 400°F. • Peel and dice tomatoes. Place diced tomatoes in pastry shell. Whisk eggs, salt, white pepper and basil together. Gradually stir in sour cream and melted butter. Pour mixture over tomatoes and sprinkle with cheese. • Bake on middle oven rack for 8 minutes. Reduce heat to 350°F and bake 25 minutes longer. • Cover filling with aluminum foil if it browns too quickly. • Serve hot.

Swiss Chard Flan

445 calories per serving
Serves: 8
Preparation time: 30 minutes
Baking time: 40 to 50 minutes

2¼ lbs. Swiss chard

12 cups water

1½ tsp. salt

7 tbs. softened butter

4 egg yolks

1 cup plus 2 tbs. low-fat ricotta or cottage cheese

½ cup whipping cream

1¼ cups flour

3 tbs. semolina

⅛ tsp. nutmeg

1 cup bread crumbs

1 cup freshly grated Swiss cheese

For the horseradish sauce:

1 large, tart apple

¼ lb. mushrooms

1 tbs. wine vinegar

2 tsp. sugar

2 tbs. freshly grated horseradish

⅛ tsp. salt

⅛ tsp. white pepper

½ cup whipping cream

Trim, sort and wash Swiss chard. Remove green leaves from stalks and cut leaves into julienne strips. Cut stalks in half lengthwise and cut into julienne strips. • Bring water and 1 teaspoon of salt to a boil in a saucepan. Add chard and blanch for 3 minutes. Drain and cool. • Preheat oven to 400° F. • Cream softened butter and egg yolks. Stir in ricotta or cottage cheese, whipping cream, flour, semolina, ½ teaspoon of salt and nutmeg. • Squeeze excess water from Swiss chard and fold into butter mixture. • Grease a 10½- inch springform pan with butter and sprinkle with ½ cup of bread crumbs. •

Spoon in chard mixture and smooth out surface with a knife. Combine remaining ½ cup of bread crumbs with grated cheese and sprinkle over flan. Bake on bottom oven rack for 40 to 50 minutes. Cover with aluminum foil if flan browns too quickly. • To make horseradish sauce, peel and grate apple. Clean and finely chop mushrooms. Combine grated apple, vinegar, sugar, horseradish, mushrooms, salt and pepper. Whip cream until stiff and fold into horseradish mixture. • Serve flan hot, with horseradish sauce.

Potato Crust Pizza

355 calories per serving
Serves: 8
Preparation time: 40 minutes
Baking time: 50 minutes

For the dough:
2¼ lbs. potatoes
1 tbs. lemon juice
Olive oil for greasing
3 eggs
½ cup whipping cream
¼ cup white wine
1 tsp. salt
⅛ tsp. sugar
1 cup freshly grated Mozzarella cheese
1 tsp. dried oregano
For the filling: 1⅓ lbs. tomatoes
7 ozs. Mozzarella cheese
2 tbs. olive oil

Peel, wash and grate potatoes. Combine with lemon juice and drain well. • Preheat oven to 400°F. Brush a pizza pan with olive oil. • Whisk eggs, whipping cream, white wine, salt, sugar, cheese and oregano together and fold into grated potatoes. Spoon potato mixture into pan. • Bake potato crust on middle rack of oven for 30 minutes. Cover with aluminum foil after 15 minutes if crust browns too quickly. • Wash, dry and slice tomatoes. Slice mozzarella cheese. • Place alternating layers of sliced tomatoes and cheese on potato crust. Sprinkle with olive oil. • Bake 20 minutes longer and serve hot.

Eggplant Pizza

260 calories per serving
Serves: 8
Preparation time: 1 hour
Baking time: 30 minutes

For the dough:

1⅔ cups flour

1 pkg. dried yeast

½ cup lukewarm water

1 tbs. olive oil

½ tsp. salt

For the filling:

⅔ lb. beef flank steak

2 tbs. olive oil

1 tsp. mixed herbs

2 cloves garlic

1⅓ lbs. eggplant

⅔ lb. tomatoes

½ tsp. salt

⅛ tsp. white pepper

1 cup freshly grated Mozzarella cheese

1 tbs. butter

Olive oil for greasing

Combine first 5 ingredients to make a yeast dough, following instructions for Onion Flan (see Index). • Slice flank steak into ½-inch wide strips. Combine olive oil and herbs, pour over meat and marinate for 20 minutes. • Peel, chop and crush garlic cloves. Slice eggplant and tomatoes. • Preheat oven to 400°F. Grease a 12-inch pizza pan with olive oil. • Roll out yeast dough and line bottom of pan with it, making a slightly higher rim around edge of dough. • Arrange steak strips, eggplant and tomato slices on pizza crust. Sprinkle with salt, white pepper, crushed garlic and meat marinade. Sprinkle Mozzarella cheese over pizza and dot with butter. • Bake for 30 minutes and serve hot.

Artichoke Flan

315 calories per serving
Serves: 8
Preparation time: 1 hour
Baking time: 30 minutes

For the dough:

1⅔ cups flour

1 pkg. dried yeast

Scant ½ cup lukewarm water

1 tbs. olive oil

⅛ tsp. salt

For the filling:

7 ozs. canned tuna

1 small clove garlic

½ tsp. salt

1 tbs. olive oil

1 tsp. dried thyme

⅛ tsp. white pepper

16 freshly cooked artichoke hearts

2 tbs. small capers

Olive oil for greasing

⅓ cup freshly grated Parmesan cheese

2 egg yolks

3 tbs. sour cream

Combine first 5 ingredients to form a yeast dough, following instructions for Onion Flan (see Index). • Drain tuna and separate into flakes. Peel and finely chop garlic, sprinkle with salt and crush with a fork. Combine crushed garlic, olive oil, thyme and pepper and pour over tuna. • Quarter artichoke hearts. • Preheat the oven to 400°F. Grease a pizza pan with olive oil. • Line bottom and sides of pizza pan with dough. Arrange artichoke hearts on dough and sprinkle with capers. Distribute tuna fish between artichoke pieces and capers. Combine Parmesan cheese, egg yolks and sour cream and pour over pizza. • Bake for 30 minutes and serve hot.

Zucchini Quiche
(left photograph)

425 calories per serving
Serves: 8
Preparation time: 20 minutes
Baking time: 40 minutes

For the dough:

| 2 cups flour |
| 1 egg yolk |
| 7 tbs. margarine |
| 1 tsp. salt |
| 2 to 4 tbs. water |

For the filling:

| 1¾ lbs. zucchini |
| 2 cloves garlic |
| 2 large onions |
| 2 tbs. olive oil |
| 2 tbs. watercress leaves |
| ¼ cup chopped chervil |
| 3 eggs |
| 7 tbs. sour cream |
| 1 cup flour |
| 3 tbs. margarine |

Preheat oven to 400°F. • Mix flour, egg yolk, margarine and salt together. Add enough water to knead mixture to make a dough. Roll out dough and line bottom and sides of a tart pan. • Bake for 15 minutes. • Wash and thinly slice zucchini. Peel garlic and onions and dice finely. • Heat olive oil in a frying pan. Add onions and garlic and sauté until onions are transparent. Add zucchini and stir-fry for 5 minutes. Remove from heat and add herbs. • Pour vegetables into pastry shell. Combine eggs and sour cream and pour over zucchini. Sprinkle with flour and dot with margarine. • Bake for 25 minutes and serve hot.

Endive Quiche
(right photograph)

305 calories per serving
Serves: 8
Preparation time: 20 minutes
Baking time: 40 to 45 minutes

For the dough:

| 2 cups flour |
| 1 egg yolk |
| 1 tsp. salt |
| 7 tbs. margarine |
| 2 to 4 tbs. water |

For the filling:

| 1¾ lbs. chicory |
| 1 red pepper |
| 2 tbs. lemon juice |
| 1 tsp. maple syrup |
| 2 tbs. chopped parsley |
| 2 eggs |
| 1 tsp. salt |
| ½ cup sour cream |
| ⅓ cup freshly grated Swiss cheese |
| 2 tbs. margarine |

Preheat oven to 400°F. • Knead flour, egg yolk, salt, margarine and enough water together to make a dough. Line a tart pan with dough. Bake for 15 minutes. • Wash endive and cut into julienne strips. Trim, wash and dice pepper, removing membrane and seeds. Combine pepper, endive, lemon juice, syrup and parsley. • Whisk eggs, salt and sour cream together, then mix in grated cheese. • Place vegetable mixture in pastry shell. Pour in egg and cream mixture and dot with margarine. • Bake quiche for 25 to 30 minutes and serve warm.

Asparagus Quiche

310 calories per serving
Serves: 8
Preparation time: 30 minutes
Baking time: 30 minutes

1⅔ lbs. green asparagus
8 cups water
1½ tsp. salt
1 tsp. sugar
2 cups flour
1 egg yolk
7 tbs. margarine
2 to 4 tbs. cold water
2 eggs
½ cup whipping cream
¼ cup freshly grated Mozzarella cheese

Thinly peel bottom part of asparagus spears, cut off woody ends, and wash aspara-gus. Tie asparagus into 4 bunches with kitchen twine. • Place 8 cups of water, 1 teaspoon of salt and sugar in a saucepan and bring to a boil. Add asparagus bunches, cover and simmer for 10 minutes. • To make the dough, sift flour onto a bread board. Quickly knead in egg yolks, ½ teaspoon of salt, margarine and just enough cold water to make a smooth dough. • Roll out dough and line bottom and sides of a quiche pan with it. • Drain asparagus spears on a paper towel. Cut asparagus spears into 2-inch pieces and arrange in pastry shell. • Whisk eggs, whipping cream and grated cheese together and pour over asparagus. • Bake for 30 minutes and serve warm.

Broccoli Quiche

265 calories per serving
Serves: 8
Preparation time: 35 minutes
Baking time: 30 minutes

1⅔ lbs. broccoli
8 cups water
1½ tsp. salt
2 cups flour
1 egg yolk
3 tbs. butter
2 to 4 tbs. cold water
7 ozs. smoked ham
2 eggs
7 ozs. sour cream
1 tsp. chopped fresh basil

Wash and trim broccoli and divide into florets. Place 8 cups of water and 1 teaspoon of salt in a saucepan and bring to a boil. Add broccoli and blanch for 7 minutes. Drain and set aside to cool. • Knead flour, egg yolk, ½ teaspoon of salt, butter and 2 to 4 tablespoons of cold water together to make a dough. Line bottom and sides of a quiche pan with dough. • Preheat oven to 400°F. • Dice ham and spread in pastry shell. Cover with broccoli. Whisk eggs, salt to taste and sour cream together. Stir in basil and pour mixture over broccoli. • Bake on middle oven rack for 30 minutes and serve warm.

Index